Proverbial Tree

Proverbial Tree

African Proverbs
and
Biblical Scriptures

Jack L. Bynum

Dedication

This book is dedicated to all of my ancestors and family in Africa, America, the diaspora, and especially to my children, LaWanda, Christina (deceased), Yolanda, Cheryl, LaDetra, and Diamond.

Introduction

As a young child, I was always fascinated by stories about Africa. For as long as I can remember, Africa was called "the motherland." Also, my first recollection of the study of world history and science was the statement that man first originated in Africa.

I cannot recall a time when most individuals in my circle were saying things that would cause me to question the existence of God. However, in the fourth grade, I seriously examined and began asking lots of questions about things I did not understand. That was around the time a classmate decided it was time for me to know more about Santa Claus. Wow! Santa had so many attributes and qualities that were similar to those referencing God. What was I to believe? Well, even at that early age, I had dreams that convinced me that God indeed exists.

In the tenth grade, I remember getting my only C for a grading period. In history I responded to a question about creation and evolution. I do not remember the exact question, but I know the textbook answer was evolution. I gave the correct answer and added to it "according to the textbook." Then I proceeded to give the Bible account of creation, and I made it known that was what I believed. I was penalized! I still believe in creation, but I can understand the position of evolutionists. It would be great if they could understand the phrase "in the eyes of God, a day is as a thousand years." If so, I think they would find it easier to relate to my position.

Since history and the Bible intersect and confirm each other in so many ways, I appreciate comparisons of information from both sources. Further, it is interesting, at the least, that in many cases there is evidence that history and the Bible draw from the same source documents. Therefore, as I learned African proverbs, I realized some of them were similar to Bible statements. I began writing and doing oral presentations on "African Proverbs and Biblical Scriptures." Then I decided to put some of my presentations and writings together in the form of a book.

The book was not created to do a historical or critical analysis of either African proverbs or Bible Scriptures. It simply shows comparisons by paralleling the two with personal comments or reflections. Each reader will need to determine for themselves how they are affected by the African proverbs and Bible Scriptures. I find relevance and practical use from both. Also, I appreciate the cultural and spiritual expansion of my horizons as I learn more.

I chose the title *Proverbial Tree*, as I thought of the tree of life, the depth of the roots of some trees, sustenance received from trees needed by mankind, and the long lives of some trees. Also, I thought of the references in the Bible to leaves and healing. Application of what is learned from both African proverbs and biblical Scriptures can make life more abundant. As an African American and Christian, my roots run deep in both. Therefore, I stand firm and enjoy the beauty and splendor of all that God has created! I sincerely hope you will enjoy the reading of *Proverbial Tree*.

Acholi Proverbs

———————— and ————————

Biblical Scriptures

"A dog knows the places he is thrown food."
(Acholi proverb)

"And she said, Truth, Lord: yet the dogs eat of the crumbs which fall from their masters' table."
(Matthew 15:27)

Comments:

It is worth noting that in most biblical references, the mentioning of dogs had far greater meanings than simply furry pets. In the reference above, the Canaanite woman used the reference to make a point regarding her faith. She knew the Jews looked upon her as less than a dog, but she was confident God looked at her heart and would not be a respecter of her person but of her faith. In any event, the woman referenced dogs knowing where to get food (even if just the crumbs). Likewise, her statement of faith was saying that although a Canaanite woman was not considered worthy of what was reserved for the Jews, she had enough faith to know that if Jesus would just respond in the manner that masters do to their dogs, if Jesus simply gave her leftovers (crumbs), that would be sufficient to meet her needs. Because she knew her source and had faith, Jesus granted her request.

Likewise, every believer should be aware that our Master (Jesus) is heir to everything. As brothers and sisters, we are heirs and joint heirs. Therefore, we should be fully aware of the source of our provisions. As written in Psalm 121:1–2, *"I will lift up mine eyes unto the hills, from whenc e c om eth m y help. My help cometh from the LORD, which m ad e heaven and earth."*

Like the Canaanite woman, believers should have faith and be fully confident that this same Jesus is ready, willing, and able to meet all of our needs. Moreover, our knowledge of God's Word increases our faith. Therefore, the promises of God have demonstrated over and over again that we don't have to settle for the crumbs. Furthermore, since God is omnipotent, omnipresent, and omniscient (all-powerful, all being, and all-knowing), our source is infinite.

African Proverbs

——————— and ———————

Biblical Scriptures

"If you are filled with pride,
then you will have no room for wisdom."
(African proverb)

"When pride cometh, then cometh shame:
but with the lowly is wisdom."
(Proverbs 11:2)

"The fear of the Lord is to hate evil:
Pride and arrogancy, and the evil way, and
the forward mouth, do I hate."
(Proverbs 8:13)

"A man's pride shall bring him low: But honour
shall uphold the humble in spirit."
(Proverbs 29:23)

"But He giveth more grace. Wherefore He saith, God
resisteth the proud, but giveth grace unto the humble."
(James 4:6)

"How art thou fallen from heaven, O Lucifer, son of the morning! How art thou cut down to the ground, which didst weaken the nations! For thou hast said in thine heart, I will ascend into heaven, I will exalt my throne above the stars of God: I will sit also upon the mount of the congregation, in the sides of the north: I will ascend above the heights of the clouds; I will be like the Most High. Yet thou shalt be brought down to hell, to the sides of the pit."
(Isaiah 14:12–15)

Read Revelation 9:9–12 and Ezekiel 28:14–17.

Comments:

One of the major problems with pride is that it distorts thinking. When filled with pride, one is unable to accept wisdom and lacks understanding. The individual's values are displaced. He or she begins to focus on things such as what others may think about them and their achievements.

When one is obsessed with personal achievements, he or she begins to exhibit a false sense of pride and dignity. Sometimes, the individual begins to feel that they are better than others. It is well to know that we can do nothing without God. We should be humble and know that God is not a respecter of persons. We were all made in His likeness and image.

Since all wisdom and knowledge comes from God, He should get the glory for all of our achievements and successes. We should be grateful for every blessing He sends our way. In addition, our thankfulness should extend to the blessings He provides to others. Be thankful for all achievements, but all of the glory belongs to God.

Note: In Isaiah 14:12–15, Lucifer says five times, "I will..." Each time he is expressing pride and saying how he will exalt himself above God. God does not share His glory with anyone. In numerous Scriptures, we are informed that we are to be humble. We are also made aware that pride comes before a fall. Prior to Lucifer's fall or being cast out of heaven, he exalted himself and tried to get above God. Also, he imposed his pride on other angels who fell with him.

I hope Lucifer's (also called Satan, the devil, and the evil one) fall will be a reminder to each of us that we are to be humble. As you read your Bible, you will find examples of individuals who fell as a result of pride. In addition, if you watch the news and read your newspaper, you will find further examples.

"By crawling a child learns to stand."
(African proverb)

"When I was a child, I spake as a child, I understood as a child, I thought as a child: but when I became a man, I put away childish things."
(1 Corinthians 13:11)

"For when for the time ye ought to be teachers, ye have need that one teach you again which be the first principles of the oracles of God; and are become such as have need of milk, and not of strong meat."
(Hebrews 5:12)

Read 1 Corinthians 3:1–5.

Comments:

Beginning at infancy, individuals develop and mature as they progress from one stage in life to another. In each stage there are measurable changes in development. Therefore, as an infant progresses to being a toddler, we expect changes in physical growth, mental capacity, speech, and behavioral changes. The same applies as one goes from being a toddler to early childhood, from early childhood to puberty, and so on to adulthood. It is unacceptable in society for adults to conduct themselves as children.

The same applies in the spiritual lives of individuals. Mature Christians should not behave as babes in Christ. As they grow and develop spiritually, a closer walk with Christ should be evident. Childish babbling, negative attitudes, bitterness, envy, and other traits that are not conducive to Christian living should be put behind them. They should strive for Christian maturity as they lay aside every weight or sin that might interfere with their fellowship with God or man.

ᘖᔍᕈᘘ

"If you close your eyes to facts,
you will learn by accident."
(African proverb)

"Ever learning, and never able to come
to the knowledge of the truth."
(2 Timothy 3:7)

Read Mark 3:17–19, Ephesians1:18–21, and
Philippians 4:11–13.

Comments:

Have you ever met individuals who think they know everything but never have facts to back anything? In many cases, it appears those individuals find it easier to believe a lie over the truth. There are some, however, who simply fail to utilize credible source materials and just miss the facts. Finally, there are those who are ever learning and are never able to make practical applications to life situations.

It is imperative that we seek the truth. When we close our eyes to the facts, what we learn by accident may be preceded by or succeeded by negative and/or detrimental consequences.

"It takes a village to raise a child."
(African proverb)

"Train up a child in the way he should go: and when he is old, he will not depart from it."
(Proverbs 22:6)

"He that spareth his rod hateth his son: But he that loveth him chasteneth him betimes."
(Proverbs 13:24)

Read Psalm 127:3–5.

Comments:

The whole village has influence on a child as it develops and matures. The environment plays a great part in how the individual develops. Also, one learns from his or her surroundings. Neither the African proverb nor the biblical Scripture mean or imply that every child will always adhere to everything they learned or to the way they were trained. However, the way individuals are trained has a profound influence on how they respond to life's situations and circumstances. Further, as they get older, it is unlikely that they will forget their training.

African Proverbs and Biblical Scriptures

"If you want to go quickly, go alone;
if you want to go far, go together."
(African proverb)

"Two are better than one; because they have a good
reward for their labour. For if they fall, the one will lift
up his fellow: but woe to him that is alone when he
falleth; for he hath not another to help him up."
(Ecclesiastes 4:9–10)

Comments:

We need each other. There are so many things we can do better in pairs or in groups that we could not accomplish alone. If neither of you fall, just think of the other ways you may be able to assist each other. For example, you may need help warding off a foe. Objects or obstructions may be a hindrance for one in cases where if there are two or more, it may be easy to overcome. Also, it is good to have company for moral support, love, joy, and the pleasures of life.

I often think of Psalm 133 which reminds us that it is good for brothers to dwell together in unity. Life is most enjoyable when we have family, friends, and loved ones to share in the things we do.

I grew up in a large family. I had eight brothers and four sisters. Most of my childhood, both parents were present. Sometimes, some of my nieces and nephews were present. Therefore, I have always enjoyed what I term "good noise." Now, some of my better days are those when my five daughters (and their significant others) seven grandchildren, and three great-grandchildren get together for family day. I am eternally grateful and thank God for every addition to the family.

Joys are similar when I have opportunities to assemble with extended family, friends, coworkers, and especially my church family. We find so many things to do together, including, traveling, singing, dancing, games, and so many other things. It is a blessing to eat together and just laugh and fellowship. All of the beautiful things God has created for our enjoyment and pleasure seem to be better when we experience them together in community.

"If relatives help each other, what evil can hurt them?"
(African proverb)

Read the books of Ruth and Esther in the Old Testament of the Bible.

Comments:

The books of Ruth and Esther in the Holy Bible are prime examples of the importance of families working together and supporting each other. In addition, there are numerous accounts throughout the Holy Bible illustrating and emphasizing lessons to be learned that will make life more joyful, peaceful, and productive when relatives help each other.

The lessons can be beneficial to us today. One only needs to ask God for help as he or she practically applies these lessons in everyday situations and circumstances.

"Children are the reward of life."
(African proverb)

"Lo, children are an heritage of the LORD:
And the fruit of the womb is His reward.
As arrows are in the hand of a mighty
man; So are children of the youth.
Happy is the man that hath his quiver full
of them: They shall not be ashamed,
But they shall speak with the enemy in the gate."
(Psalm 127:3–5)

Read Psalm 24:1–2.

Comments:

God is our Creator. As Psalm 24:1–2 informs us that the earth, the fullness of the earth, and everyone that dwells on earth belongs to Him. He is the giver and sustainer of life. The children or offspring that He gives us are an heritage to us. Children are the special allotment or possession that He passes down from generation to generation. Throughout the Bible, children are identified as a blessing from God.

God makes us aware that children are rewards from Him with the many miraculous births He granted to those who were barren or beyond childbearing age. Children are precious! They add joy and happiness to our lives. Think of the women and men in the Bible who prayed for years that God would grant them this precious gift of children.

Proverbial Tree

"Hold a true friend with both hands."
(African proverb)

"Between true friends even water drunk together is sweet enough."
(African proverb)

"A friend is someone you share the path with."
(African proverb)

"Greater love hath no man than this, that a man lay down his life for his friends."
(John 15:13)

"A friend loveth at all times, and a brother is born for adversity."
(Proverbs 17:17)

"A man that hath friends must shew himself friendly: And there is a friend that sticketh closer than a brother."
(Proverbs 18:24)

Read Philippians 4:8. Also, read 1 Samuel: 20.

Comments:

One of my favorite Bible accounts of friendship is found in 1 Samuel. In chapter 20, David and Jonathan make a friendship oath based on their faith in God. The friendship illustrated by these two individuals was so strong that Jonathan was even willing to forsake the wishes and commands of his father, King Saul. It is rare that one finds a friend of this magnitude. Jonathan even risked his life in some cases to save David.

As I reflected on the African proverbs and Scriptures above, I could not help taking a retrospective look at the rekindling of a friendship which withstood the test of approximately forty-five years of separation. I had a close friendship with an individual, Robert Powell, from fifth grade through tenth grade. At the end of our sophomore year in high school, we were separated as a result of busing and high school integration.

Over forty-five years later, he was inquiring about me at a church function. The person he communicated with informed him I was blind (Note: His father became visually impaired while he was still in high school). The person he talked with had previously had one of my brothers, Woody, to do some work for him. Robert requested the telephone number of my brother and finally made contact with me

My friend has to drive approximately three hundred miles to visit me. However, he makes the drive two to three times per month and checks on me. This is especially significant to me because I have zero vision and live alone. He does not just check on me, but he also ensures that while he is in the area, I get to take care of many of the basic needs that would otherwise be difficult, at the least. In addition, when I can get over my fear of riding with him, we visit friends, family, churches, and social and recreational events. I mention him specifically because there are few local friends (and even fewer individuals who identify themselves as brothers and sisters in Christ) who make the same sacrifices.

Finally, this friendship is unique because I accepted Christ over five decades ago. I have been an ordained minister for almost forty years. When this friend contacted me around three years ago, he did not consider himself as a brother in Christ. Today, Robert is my brother and friend and is currently looking for his church home. I give God all the glory, honor, and praise for true friends.

*"Show me your friends and I will show you
your character."*
(African proverb)

*"For a good tree bringeth not forth corrupt fruit; neither
doth a corrupt tree bring forth good fruit. For every
tree is known by his own fruit. For of thorns men do not
gather figs, nor of a bramble bush gather they grapes. A
good man out of the good treasure of his heart bringeth
forth that which is good; and an evil man out of the evil
treasure of his heart bringeth forth that which is evil: For
of the abundance of the heart the mouth speaketh."*
(Luke 6:43–45)

"Can two walk together, except they be agreed?"
(Amos 3:3)

Comments:

Have you ever heard the saying "Birds of a feather flock together"? The practical application of the phrase to man is that people of similar character usually associate with one another. In Amos 3:3, the implication is the same. People often choose friends who like the same things as themselves. That is probably the reason people are sometimes assumed to be guilty by association.

Generally, we associate with individuals who share our character traits. We would not expect a person of good moral character to intentionally choose as his friend a bank robber.

"It's those ugly caterpillars that turn into
beautiful butterflies after seasons."
(African proverb)

"And be not conformed to this world:
but be ye transformed by the renewing of your
mind, that ye may prove what is that good, and
acceptable, and perfect, will of God."
(Romans 12:2)

Read Romans 12:1.

"Therefore if any man be in Christ, he is a new creature:
old things are passed away; behold,
all things are become new."
(2 Corinthians 5:17)

**Read 1 Kings 8:37, 2 Chronicles 6:28, Psalm 78:46,
and Isaiah 33:4.**

Comments:

In the Old Testament Scriptures listed above, the caterpillar is recognized as a destructive creature which devours vegetation and plant life. Therefore, the caterpillar, along with the locust, was recognized as destructive creatures that contributed to many of the famines of the times. As a result, the caterpillar was thought of as ugly.

Amazingly, the caterpillar, after a season, goes through a stage called metamorphosis, (a transformation) and becomes a beautiful butterfly. As a butterfly, it is neither ugly nor destructive.

Instead, the butterfly aids in the pollination of flowers, which contributes to the process of reproduction of vegetation, flowers, and other plant life.

Likewise, in the New Testament Scriptures mentioned above, we are informed of the transformation of man into a new creature. After a season, that is, acceptance of Christ as Savior, man loses his old sinful (ugly) nature and transforms into a new (beautiful) creature with a renewed mind to serve God. After the transformation, the new man no longer has a desire to conform to the things of this world. Instead, he makes Jesus his choice and strives to do the will of God.

ᘒᘏᕘᕓ

"Nobody is born wise."
(African proverb)

Read 1 Kings 3, Proverbs 1:7, and Psalm 90:12.

Comments:

Throughout the Bible, we are instructed how to attain wisdom. In 1 Kings 3, Solomon asked God for wisdom. We are reminded in numerous biblical accounts that wisdom is given by God.

Since Jesus is omnipotent, omniscient, and omnipresent, He is "from everlasting to everlasting" (infinite). Therefore, He was born wise. Others attained their wisdom through training (learning), experience, and/or by gifts from God. Ultimately, even the training and experiences are by the gracious gifts of God.

Proverbial Tree

"To get lost is to learn the way."
(African proverb)

"For the Son of Man is come to seek
and to save that which was lost."
(Luke 19:10)

**Read Luke 15:11–32. This is the Parable of
the Prodigal Son. Read Matthew 15:24.**

Comments:

In the Parable of the Prodigal Son, the son who thought he knew everything did not learn his way until he got lost, that is, until he realized he did not know it all. It was at this point that he came to the realization that he did not know the way. Therefore, he returned home to a loving father who knew the way.

How many times have you thought you knew the way or exactly what you were doing, only to find out later you did not have a clue? That is why our priority should be first to seek Christ and His righteousness.

ಉಂ೪ಲಿ

"The wise create proverbs for fools to learn,
not to repeat."
(African proverb)

**Read Proverbs 1. Then read all of the book of
Proverbs. In addition, proverbs, maxims, and wisdom
sayings can be found throughout the Bible.**

Comments:

In order for Proverbs to help individuals in life's situations and circumstances, it is important that people do more than just repeat them. In order for the Proverbs to be beneficial, individuals must learn and utilize them through practical application.

"What you help a child to love can be more important than what you help him to learn."
(African proverb)

"Even a child is known by his doings, whether his work be pure, and whether it be right."
(Proverbs 20:11)

Comments:

It is important to teach a child. However, if the child is not taught to love what he learns, he may not put what he learns to practical use.

When I was a child, and during early adulthood, my older brother taught me a lot about auto mechanics. I did not enjoy working on cars and never made much use of what I learned. On the other hand, I loved music and applied what I learned in high school and from high school graduation to the present in many ways.

One of the earliest things I was taught to memorize was the twenty-fourth Psalm. That was the beginning of my love for the Bible. I have enjoyed the Word of God continuously after that experience. It led to an undergraduate degree in religion and a master's in divinity. I have been in ministry for over fifty years and an ordained elder for over four decades. I love it!

"What you learn is what you die with."
(African proverb)

"Precious in the sight of the Lord
is the death of his saints."
(Psalm 116:15)

Read Psalm 116:15–17.

"For to me to live is Christ, and to die is gain."
(Philippians 16:15)

"The fear of the Lord prolongeth days:
but the years of the wicked shall be shortened."
(Proverbs 10:27)

"And we know that all things work together
for good to them that love God, to them who
are the called according to His purpose."
(Romans 8:28)

Read Romans 8:28–39.

**Read Ecclesiastes 3:1–8 and 7:17, Philippians 1:21–26,
and 1 Thessalonians 4:13–18.**

Reflections:

When I was a child, there was a song that I learned that has been a blessing to me from the moment I learned it. The title of the song was "Everybody Ought to Know Who Jesus Is." When you know Jesus, it seems that every day truly gets "Sweeter Than the Day Before" (the title of another song). In 2007, the earthly life of one of my brothers, Clifton, ended. Even though I saw the daily demise of his physical body, the day of his transition was somewhat shocking, at least for a few minutes. He was laying on the bed, and we were having a joyful conversation. There were only four people present. My brother, Clifton, his wife, Un Suk "Sandy," my sister, Sudie, and myself were all laughing, conversing, and just having a great time. However, in the midst of the conversation Clifton said to me, "Lift my hands." I was not certain I understood him, so I asked, "What did you say?" He replied, "Never mind." Then he fell silent for a few moments. His wife stepped out on the front porch, and I followed behind her.

My sister, Sudie, remained in the room with Clifton. Less than one minute after I stepped on the porch, my sister stood in the door and said, "He is gone." She said he also asked her to lift his hands. She said she did so, and as soon as his hands were lifted, they dropped back down, and with a smile, he breathed his last breath.

I do not know how many people can identify with what happened, or if I can adequately articulate it in a comprehensible manner. Suffice it to say, it was one of the most beautiful moments in my life. I cannot imagine a more beautiful departure or transition to be with the Lord. The only thing I can think of that would be comparable in beauty would be if one were caught up like Elijah. There was a beauty and peace that surpasses all understanding.

It is so good to learn and know the Lord. Can you imagine anything more beautiful than to know Him in such a way that when it is time for your earthly departure, you are full of joy and peace?

I can imagine my brother seeing and having knowledge of "the beauty and splendor of all that God has created" in those final moments. No wonder, Paul, the apostle, said, "to die is gain."

"Greed loses what it has gained."
(African proverb)

"Yea, they are greedy dogs which can never have enough, and they are shepherds that cannot understand: they all look to their own way, every one for his gain, from his quarter."
(Isaiah 56:11)

"Better is the poor that walketh in his uprightness, than he that is perverse in his ways, though he be rich."
(Proverbs 28:6)

"Wealth gotten by vanity shall be diminished: but he that gathereth by labour shall increase."
(Proverbs 13:11)

Read Hebrews 13:5.

Comments:

Have you ever noticed individuals who are so greedy that they lose hard-earned money through ridiculous risks? There are individuals who earn enough to take care of their basic needs. However, they are so greedy that instead of taking care of their needs and obligations, they gamble and lose what they already had.

My dad often told his children, "A bird in the hand is worth more than two in the bush." So many times people are trying so hard to reach for more that they lose what they already have without getting what they were reaching after. They would let the bird go that they already had while reaching for the two in the bush. In most scenarios, they lose it all.

Similarly, many people will spend so much of their earnings on lottery tickets or gambling that they cannot pay their bills. Oftentimes, even if they win large sums of money, their greed causes them to risk it trying to gain more and end up broke. Moreover, some even put up what they already own outright as collateral, only to lose it by gambling.

As the world was battling the pandemic coronavirus (COVID-19), my daughter shared a story of excessive greed which caused individuals to purchase large quantities of hand sanitizer. According to her account, they made the purchases from several states and stored them in a large barn. Then they proceeded to sell them on Amazon at exorbitant prices. When Amazon became aware of what they were doing during a worldwide crisis, they refused to allow them to sell on Amazon. Therefore, they lost their investment and the products remained in the barn.

"Love never gets lost; it's only kept."
(African proverb)

Read 2 Corinthians 13:8 in the King James Version. Then read the whole chapter. Finally, read it again in other translations to get a better understanding about love and endurance.

"For God so loved the world, that He gave His only begotten Son, that whosoever believeth in Him should not perish, but have everlasting life."
(John 3:16)

Read 1 John 4:8–16 and all of Hosea.

Comments:

If you read the Holy Bible from Genesis through Revelation, you will find illustrations of God's love in every book. His love is infinite because is from everlasting to everlasting.

We should model His love. In order to do so, we must forgive each other of our transgressions. When people mistreat us, as difficult as it may seem, we should strive to forgive and love in spite of their wrongdoings.

The prophet Hosea in the book of Hosea, was an example of one who had love that never got lost. He exemplified the love that God has for us. Although he married a woman of harlotry, he had a love that continued even when she abandoned their marriage. Likewise, we abandon God over and over again. Yet, He forgives and has an everlasting love.

Proverbial Tree

꧁꧂

"However long the night, the dawn will break."
(African proverb)

"For His anger endureth but a moment;
In His favour is life:
Weeping may endure for a night,
But joy cometh in the morning."
(Psalm 30:5)

Comments:

Sometimes, it seems that trouble is all around us, and we are going through the dark storms of life. However, such times pass, and then it is like sunny days again. As we reflect on God's created handiwork, we realize that the weeping and dark times come to an end just as the night. Our awesome God created the universe in such a way that the darkest hour is just before dawn. Often, dark hours or times in life seem to come just before the dawning of great blessings from God.

Therefore, when things are not going the way we think they should, we ought to have faith that all things will work out for our good (see Romans 8:28). Know that we serve a God who loves us and has a plan for us. His plan is for good and not for evil (see Jeremiah 29:11).

*"Food gained by fraud tastes sweet to a man,
but he ends up with gravel in his mouth."*
(African proverb)

*"Bread of deceit is sweet to a man; but afterwards
his mouth shall be filled with gravel."*
(Proverbs 20:17)

Comments:

Have you ever seen on the news, television, or read articles about situations in which individuals lost their lives while trying to get food or something else by deceit, fraud, or theft? I am convinced the best way to get what we want in life is to ask God for help and work. In most societies, if you are unable to work, there are groups that will provide support for food and other things one may need.

Proverbial Tree

*"A spider's cobweb isn't only its sleeping
spring but also its food trap."*
(African proverb)

*"The spider taketh hold with her hands,
and is in kings' palaces."*
(Proverbs 30:28)

Read 1 Samuel 24.

Comments:

The spider is even wiser than implied in the above African proverb. As indicated in Proverbs 30:28, the spider is also capable of skillfully using its appendages to navigate its way into kings' palaces. In 1 Samuel 24, God uses the spider to weave a web to conceal the hideout of David in a cave. David was hiding from King Saul who was seeking to kill him.

Do you ever pause to think about how God gives wisdom to the creatures He created? As you enjoy the beauty and splendor of all that He has created, consider the many ways He uses what we may think of as insignificant or fragile to bless us every day.

Akamba Proverbs

—————— and ——————

Biblical Scriptures

"The hyena with a cub does not
consume all the available food."
(Akamba proverb)

"Behold, the third time I am ready to come to you;
and I will not be burdensome to you: for I seek not
yours but you: for the children ought not to lay up
for the parents, but the parents for the children."
(2 Corinthians 12:14)

Comments:

One of the characteristics of the hyena is a high-pitched
laughing sound when it is excited. In addition to other reasons,
this sound is made when new sources of food are located to alert
other hyenas.

Certainly, if animals of the wild know to take care of one
another, we who are considered to be superior beings ought to do

the same. In the biblical reference above, Paul the apostle informs the Corinthian church of his impending third visit. As pastor and leader (the parental role), Paul communicates that he will not expect them to take care of him, but he will strive to provide for them. Whether spiritually or physically, the parents' responsibility is to take care of the children, instead of the children taking care of the parents. I would add that like the hyena, we ought to get excited about it! We should rejoice that the amazing God that we serve provides everything that we need. Moreover, parents should be grateful that He allows us to pass some of those blessings on to the children He gave us as well as others.

Akan Proverbs

———————— and ————————

Biblical Scriptures

"Only a wise person can solve a difficult problem."
(Akan proverb)

"And God said to Solomon,
Because this was in thine heart, and thou hast not
asked riches, wealth, or honour, nor the life
of thine enemies, neither yet hast asked long
life; but hast asked wisdom and knowledge for
thyself, that thou mayest judge my people,
over whom I have made thee king."
(2 Chronicles 1:11)

Read 1 Kings 3:4–15, and then read all of 1 Kings 3.

"But of him are ye in Christ Jesus, who of God
is made unto us wisdom, and righteousness,
and sanctification, and redemption:"
(1 Corinthians 1:30)

Comments:

The Scriptures above inform us that wisdom comes from God. Further, one finds that through wisdom, one solves difficult problems. Solomon asked God for wisdom and knowledge, not for selfish reasons, but so he could rightfully judge the people over whom he was made king. Likewise, we need to realize the need for wisdom and knowledge and make our request of God.

Reflections:

My parents, Robert Samson Bynum and Rosa Lee Fuller Bynum, were tenant farmers. I was blessed to have four sisters and eight brothers. My father only had a third-grade education and my mother a tenth-grade education. Yet, they were able, with the help of God, to provide for all of us. I often think about it and wonder how they did it. I know God had to give Dad wisdom and understanding because he never learned to read. Still, there was always an abundance of food, shelter, clothing, and lots of love.

Sometimes I observe individuals who have difficulties providing for their families, even though they have college degrees. I often inform the children that God gave me that I learned more about life and how to take care of family from Dad than all of my teachers and college professors together. Many times, I have found it necessary to utilize the things Dad taught us in order to matriculate through college, as well as to provide for my five daughters. Two of my daughters were not privileged to meet my dad and the other three cannot remember him. Yet, his legacy lives on through the surviving daughters. Sometimes, when they are sharing wisdom with my grandchildren, I will smile when I hear one of them say, "Daddy said his dad always taught him…"

Ashanti Proverbs
— and —
Biblical Scriptures

*"When you follow in the path of your
father, you learn to walk like him."*
(Ashanti proverb)

*"He that saith he abideth in Him ought himself
also so to walk, even as He walked."*
(1 John 2:6)

Read 3 John 1:4 and 1 Kings 3:14.

Comments:

Were you one of those who tried to step in the same footsteps as your father? I mean literally as a child when you saw his footprints in the dirt or sand. I do not know about you, but I could be meticulous as I tried to place my feet just as he placed his feet. My feet were so small that they could never fill his footprints. Yet, I wanted to walk like him, so I practiced and tried over and over again. The more I attempted to emulate him, the closer I was able to walk like him.

Now I have children, grandchildren, and great-grandchildren. I am still trying to walk like him. He transitioned to be with the Lord many years ago. Therefore, I find myself modeling after the things he taught me and making practical applications of what I learned.

As Christians, we ought also to follow in the steps of our heavenly Father. We can walk in His steps by reading, studying, and abiding in the Word of God. The more we study and emulate Christ, the greater will be our level of maturity.

We should not just ask ourselves what Jesus would do, but we should read, study, learn, and walk like Him.

"You must act as if it is impossible to fail."
(Ashanti proverb)

*"Do not let what you cannot do tear
from your hands what you can."*
(Ashanti proverb)

*"I can do all things through Christ
which strengtheneth me."*
(Philippians 4:13)

Read Romans 8:28–29.

Read the 29ᵗʰ Chapter of Jeremiah.

*"For I know the thoughts that I think towards
you, saith the Lord, thoughts of peace, and not
of evil, to give you an expected end."*
(Jeremiah 29:11)

"Now faith is the substance of things hoped
for, the evidence of things not seen."
(Hebrews 11:1).

Comments:

God is omnipotent, omnipresent, and omniscient. In laymen's terms, He is all-powerful, all-present or all-being, and all-wise or all-knowing. He is infinite and cannot fail. As Christians, we believe He lives in us. Therefore, we ought to act as if we cannot fail. Further, if we confess Romans 8:28, whatever our situation or circumstance, we should understand that all things work together for our good.

There will certainly be times when it does not appear that things are working for our good. It is during those times that we need to know and reflect on the Word of God. One of my favorite Bible stories is the life of Joseph, the son of Jacob. God used him in miraculous ways and blessed him beyond measure. However, before he arrived at the pinnacle of his blessings, he had to ride out many storms of life. When he got to the place where God would use him the most, he realized all of the things that previously appeared to be negative only worked out for his good. Moreover, it was not just for his good, but for the prosperity and well-being of his family and future generations.

Reflections:

When my family and I are going through what we consider to be difficult times, I simply remind us to be encouraged and confident that everything will work out for our good. As we accentuate the positive in what appears to be negative, my faith is that through Christ Jesus, I cannot fail. Failure is not an option because we are more than conquerors in Christ. In all situations, victory is mine!

Have you ever known individuals who were so afraid of failure that they would not try? One of my daughters was living in a two-bedroom apartment and paying almost nine hundred dollars a month for rent. For a long time, she was afraid to purchase a home out of concern that she might not be able to make the payments. After a great deal of encouragement from others and prayer, she finally purchased a beautiful home. Her mortgage was approximately two hundred dollars less than the previous rent. In addition, she was privileged to purchase a four-bedroom house with two-and-a-half bathrooms, with a garage and fenced-in backyard. Approximately ten years later, the value of the house doubled.

I shared the above reflection because many people miss great opportunities and blessings out of fear of failure. In all things, I recommend that each person pray and seek God for guidance. But please, do not be afraid to strive for excellence or success out of fear. When fear confronts you, decree and exclaim, *"I can do all things through Chris t which strengtheneth me"* (Philippians 4:13).

Further, when I meditate on the letter Jeremiah penned to the captives (Jeremiah 29), I rejoice that God has plans for us. Therefore, my expected end is success!

ʊꙄ૧ʊ

"By the time the fool has learned the game,
the players have dispersed."
(Ashanti proverb)

"A fool hath no delight in understanding,
but that his heart may discover itself."
(Proverbs 18:2)

"A fool uttereth all his mind:
but a wise man keepeth it in till afterwards."
(Proverbs 29:11)

Read Proverbs 1:5–6.

Comments:

The African proverb above seems to imply fools catch on so slow that if they are engaged in activities with others, by the time they figure out what is happening, the event is over. I would contend that the scenario is often that the fool may be of the impression that he is enlightened when he does not have a clue.

Sometimes, as the Scriptures above note, the fool speaks what he does not know or at an inopportune time. On the other hand, a wise person limits what he says and enters conversations with appropriate responses at the right time. He knows when to speak and when to listen.

❧⸲❧

*"When a king has good counsellors,
his reign is peaceful."*
(Ashanti proverb)

*"Where no counsel is, the people fall:
but in the multitude of counsellors there is safety."*
(Proverbs 11:14)

*"For by wise counsel thou shalt make thy war: And
in multitude of counsellors there is safety."*
(Proverbs 24:6)

Read Proverbs 19:20–21.

Comments:

Have you ever known individuals who always want to make all of the decisions without any input from others? This usually generates ineffective results and poor leadership. It is good to surround oneself with others who are knowledgeable about the given subject matter. Provided an individual has wise counsel, he or she is more equipped to make better decisions.

In studying the Bible, we find that the kings that were most victorious in war sought wise counsel. They did not accept counsel from just any enlightened person, but they looked to true prophets or men of God. Likewise, if we seek God and wise counsel from His emissaries, we will make better decisions.

ᘯᏕᏕᘯ

"One cannot both feast and become rich."
(Ashanti proverb)

*"He that loveth pleasure shall be a poor man: He
that loveth wine and oil shall not be rich."*
(Proverbs 21:17)

Comments:

We should always seek balance in life. As we set our goals and objectives, one of the most important strategies is to prioritize. If we allocate all our resources to one area, there will be no resources for anything else.

Proverbial Tree

"Money is sharper than the sword."
(Ashanti proverb)

"For the love of money is the root of all evil: which while some coveted after, they have erred from the faith, and pierced themselves through with many sorrows."
(1 Timothy 6:10)

Comments:

It is imperative that when we examine or interpret the above Scripture, we do not take it out of context. Our God made the heavens, earth, the world, and everything in it. All the wealth, gold, silver, rubies, pearls, and every precious element or resource belongs to Him. He wants us to prosper spiritually and financially.

It is the "love of money" that is the root of all evil. The "love of money" causes evil individuals to do things to hurt themselves and others. It causes people to abandon, abuse, and do all manner of evil to satisfy their greed for ill-gotten gain. The love of money may even cause one to steal or kill.

ᘔᏕᏥᏥ

"The poor man and the rich man do not play together."
(Ashanti proverb)

"Wealth maketh many friends;
but the poor is separated from his neighbour."
(Proverbs 19:4)

Comments:

God is so amazing! He is not a respecter of persons. He loves us all and makes provisions for all His children.

One does not have to travel far to realize the rich do not generally play, associate together, or live in the same neighborhoods as the poor. Even when wealthy philanthropists donate monies to the less fortunate, they ascertain they are located in areas as far from them as possible. Sometimes, neighborhoods or communities undergo gentrification. This is when deteriorating communities, neighborhoods, or businesses are upgraded to make it more conformable to middle class values. Gentrification generally further displaces or separates the wealthy, middle class, and poor. The individual who is already living in poverty cannot afford the upgrades. Therefore, the result for those families or businesses is the worst, and they are displaced to even lesser living conditions.

Baluba Proverbs
———— and ————
Biblical Scriptures

"The skin of the leopard is beautiful, but not his heart"
(Baluba proverb)

"The heart is deceitful above all things, and desperately wicked: Who can know it?"
(Jeremiah 17:9)

Read 1 Samuel 16:7–11.

Comments:

It is a grave mistake to only look at the outward appearance to try to determine beauty or character. The outward appearance shows only a minimum of what ones needs know about a person.

When we accept only what we see on the outside, such as stature, physical attractiveness, or clothing, we miss what is in the heart. Therefore, so many are deceived because they allowed themselves to be captivated by fine houses, cars, clothing, physical appearance, wealth, or some other tangible object.

In 1 Samuel 16, Samuel was instructed to go to Jesse and anoint the person who was to succeed Saul as king. Jesse had eight sons. He brought each of them to Samuel based on outward appearance or who Jesse thought would be acceptable. Samuel had to refuse the first seven and inform Jesse that God looks at the heart instead of the outward appearance. Finally, when Jesse brought his last son, the one he thought would be least presentable or acceptable, Samuel informed Jesse that "this is the one."

Bateke Proverbs

_____ and _____

Biblical Scriptures

_"You learn how to cut down trees by
cutting them down."_
(Bateke proverb)

_"Study to shew thyself approved unto God,
a workman that needeth not to be ashamed,
rightly dividing the word of truth."_
(2 Timothy 2:15)

Comments:

How often have you heard the phrase "Practice makes perfect?"
It has been my experience that the more I practice (or study), the
more improvement I show in most tasks. Generally, people are
able to learn or achieve at a more rapid pace if they get hands-on
experience to accompany a learning opportunity.

Botswana Proverbs
———— and ————
Biblical Scriptures

"Beautiful words don't put porridge in the pot."
(Botswana proverb)

"For even when we were with you, this we commanded you, that if any would not work, neither should he eat."
(2 Thessalonians 3:10)

Comments:

In the Scriptural reference above, Paul the apostle was instructing the early Apostolic Church of the Jewish tradition. Within this culture, it was felt that any person not willing to work was not worthy to eat. The Botswana proverb implies the same. Beautiful words do not provide what is necessary to eat. In order to have food to eat, one must work. From the natural perspective, just think of the amount of work involved in planting and harvesting agricultural crops. Considerable work is also involved in hunting and fishing. Even after the food is acquired, preparation must be made in cleaning and cooking.

Burundian Proverbs

———— and ————

Biblical Scriptures

"Where there is love, there is no darkness."
(Burundian proverb)

"Then spake Jesus again unto them, saying, I am the light of the world: He that followeth me shall not walk in darkness, but shall have the light of life."
(John 8:12)

"God is love" and "God is light." Read 1 John 4:7–10 and 1 John 1:5–7.

Read Psalm 119:105, John 1:5, and John 8:12, Revelation 21:22–25 and Revelation 22:5.

Comments:

Love, light, and goodness are synonymous. Their opposites are hate, darkness, and evil. If one thinks of light and darkness in regards to illumination, it is a natural phenomenon that light and darkness cannot occupy the same space at the same time. When you enter a dark room and turn on the light, the light illuminates the room and darkness disappears.

The Bible informs us that "God is love and God is light." The Scriptures enlighten individuals that love and light always outshine and overcome evil and darkness. As love fills our hearts, sin and evil or darkness can no longer dwell in us. The Light (God) abides in us as we abide in Him. We are illuminated from the inside out, and sin, darkness, hate, and evil have no place in our lives.

Cameroon Proverbs

———————— and ————————

Biblical Scriptures

"The heart of the wise man lies quiet like limpid water."
(Cameroon proverb)

*"Counsel in the heart of man is like deep water,
but a man of understanding will draw it out."*
(Proverbs 20:5)

Comments:

Wise men have a tremendous capacity of wisdom, knowledge, and understanding. They may have deep thoughts, but they are intelligent enough to know that it is unwise to share everything. Regardless to their transparency, it is difficult to determine what is in the depths of their hearts. However, if they are willing to engage with another person of wisdom, that individual can likely draw from the deep, calm, and even obscure parts of the man's heart and draw out understanding.

Proverbial Tree

"A man's wealth may be superior to him."
(Cameroon proverb)

"Knowledge is better than riches."
(Cameroon proverb)

*"A good name is rather to be chosen than great riches,
and loving favour rather than silver and gold."*
(Proverbs 22:1)

*"And by knowledge shall the chambers be filled
with all precious and pleasant riches."*
(Proverbs 24:4)

Read Proverbs 3:13–15, 4:7, and 18:16.

**Read Ecclesiastes 6, in its entirety.
Then read Ecclesiastes 7:12.**

Read 1 Timothy 6:10.

Comments:

In the first Cameroon proverb above, there is an indication that an individual may be inferior to his or her wealth. So many people spend the majority of their lives seeking wealth or material gain. Unfortunately, many of these individuals are unable to enjoy the wealth after they have amassed it. Further, they are full of greed and hoard their wealth, not understanding the need or blessing they get from sharing. They lack the knowledge and comprehension that our blessings come from God through the wisdom and divine favor He imputes to us.

The Scriptures, along with the Cameroon Proverbs, remind the reader of the importance of knowledge and wisdom. God's favor is one of the greatest gifts to possess. Through His favor, wisdom, knowledge, and understanding are granted. With these gifts, spiritual and physical riches and wealth will follow. Upon receiving the riches, one will know how to share, enjoy, and give God glory and honor for all His blessings.

God is our Creator, and everything belongs to Him (Psalm 24:1). It would be such a blessing to all mankind if everyone could come to this realization. I belong to God and everything He blesses me to enjoy. Therefore, one of my greatest joys is to experience others enjoying the beauty and splendor of His creation.

உௐௐ

"She is like a road, pretty—but crooked."
(Cameroon proverb)

Read Proverbs 2:10–22.

Comments:

There are references throughout the Bible providing descriptions of crooked women. Usually, they identified as harlots or false brides. They are full of deceit and cause individuals to lose their spiritual gifts and rewards. The pernicious influences of crooked women have led to the downfall of individuals, families, communities, nations, and kingdoms.

Congolese Proverbs
———————— and ————————
Biblical Scriptures

*"You are beautiful but learn to work for
you cannot eat your beauty."*
(Congolese proverb)

"When the leg does not walk, the stomach does not eat."
(Congolese proverb)

Read 1 Samuel 16:7–11.

*"For even when we were with you, this we commanded
you, that if any would not work, neither should he eat."*
(2 Thessalonians 3:10)

Comments:

When it is necessary to provide for our nourishment and
sustenance, nothing supplants the need to work. All able-
bodied individuals are expected to work to provide for food for

themselves and their families. In both the Congolese proverbs and the Scriptures above, statements of what was expected by cultural norms and traditions was presented to the readers.

*"You do not teach the paths of the forest
to an old gorilla."*
(Congolese proverb)

*"I have written unto you, fathers, because ye have
known Him that is from the beginning. I have written
unto you, young men, because ye are strong,
and the Word of God abideth in you, and
ye have overcome the wicked one."*
(1 John 2:14)

Comments:

Once tasks have been learned and practiced over a period of time, it is not generally necessary to teach them again. In the Congolese proverb, the old gorilla probably helped build the path. He probably traveled it many times over and taught young gorillas how to navigate through the forest.

Paul makes it known that he is aware of the knowledge the fathers have already received. Therefore, it is probably not a matter of teaching them but refreshing their memories and encouraging them. According to Paul, they have known Him from the beginning.

"The friends of our friends are our friends."
(Congolese proverb)

*"A man that hath friends must shew himself friendly: And
there is a friend that sticketh closer than a brother."*
(Proverbs 18:24)

*"This is my commandment, that ye love one another,
as I have loved you. Greater love hath no man than
this, that a man lay down his life for his friends. Ye are
my friends, if ye do whatsoever I command you.
Henceforth I call you not servants; for the servant
knoweth not what his Lord doeth: but I have called you
friends; for all things that I have heard of my Father
I have made known unto you."*
(John 15:12–15)

Reflections:

There was a man who was incarcerated for twenty-eight years. When he was finally released from prison, he wanted to change environments. A friend who he met when he was in prison invited him to move approximately two hundred and fifty miles from his hometown to live with him. He moved in with the friend for about three years until he got married (that is, the one who had been incarcerated). His marriage lasted eleven years, and he found himself homeless. That same friend welcomed him back into his home again. However, this time, a few days after he moved in, his probation officer made a visit and told him he could no longer live at his friend's residence. He had to move out the same day because the house was too close to a daycare center. The former inmate was facing a dilemma because he had no money. However, when friends have friends, help is not far removed.

Before the former prisoner arrived from work that day, his friend had called another friend who barely knew the former inmate. However, because he was the friend of a friend, he was welcomed into the home of the friend who barely knew him. It only took a phone call making the individual aware of the situation.

The third-party friend welcomed the former prisoner into his home for five months without any charges or financial obligations. After the five months were over, the friend (former inmate) continued living in the home of the third-party friend for six months with minimal financial contributions. When he finally found a residence where he would be living independently, the third-party friend gave him a bed, two sets of bed linens, two comforters, bathroom accessories, a table and two chairs (for his kitchen), financial support, and other household items.

As indicated in Proverbs 18:24, there are friends who stick closer than brothers. God commands that we love one another. Love and friendship should be shown, not just spoken.

Egyptian Proverbs
— and —
Biblical Scriptures

"A beautiful thing is never perfect."
(Egyptian proverb)

"But the Lord said unto Samuel, look not on his countenance, or on the height of his stature; because I have refused him: For the Lord seeth not as man seeth; for man looketh on the outward appearance, but the Lord looketh on the heart."
(1 Samuel 16:7)

Read 1 Samuel 16:7–13.

Comments:

How many times have you purchased something you thought was beautiful, only to find out it was flawed after you inspected it further when you got home? Perhaps it was clothing, household items, a car, or something else you thought was perfect. It is easy to overlook the flaws in things that appeal to us. Sometimes, the problem is that we focus on a particular part or feature that is so attractive.

We encounter the same problem when we focus on the wrong things in people. We often look at their physical appearance or countenance. We may focus on materialistic things, such as clothing, jewelry, or other tangible things.

It is good to know that God is not like man. As we learn in 1 Samuel 16, God looks at our hearts. Man sees the camouflage of what shows up from our outward appearance. Therefore it is difficult for man to know or see the real person.

"Youth is beauty, even in cattle."
(Egyptian proverb)

"The glory of young men is their strength, and the beauty of old men is the gray head."
(Proverbs 20:29)

Comments:

Many people fail to see the beauty in older individuals. As one ages, his or her steps may get shorter; they may begin to wrinkle; they may lose hair; and their health may decline; but they are still beautiful. There is an inner beauty that comes with wisdom, knowledge, experience, and maturity. Let us not only see the beauty in youth, but in all of God's creation!

Ethiopian Proverbs
— and —
Biblical Scriptures

The fool speaks; the wise man listens."
(Ethiopian proverb)

"A fool uttereth all his mind:
But a wise man keepeth it in till afterwards."
(Proverbs 29:11)

"A wise man will hear, and will increase learning; and a
man of understanding shall attain unto wise counsels:
To understand a proverb, and the interpretation;
the words of the wise, and their dark sayings."
(Proverbs 1:5–6).

Comments:

One of the ideal characteristics of proverbs, maxims, and wisdom sayings is that they are simple enough so most people can understand them. When I read the above Ethiopian proverb,

I immediately thought of the number of times I have heard an individual speak about something without having adequate knowledge of the subject or topic. Sometimes, I believe they were aware of their ignorance and simply attempted to deceive others with a lot of nonsensible words. Time and time again, they are the fast talkers who suppose others are impressed with many words. The result of such communications show the foolishness or ignorance of people.

The wise man, however, usually spends more time listening and learning. He or she does not feel the need to try to impress others with their wisdom. They know when to speak and when to listen. As a result, even when the wise man lacks information or facts about a matter, one will not know unless he tells you. If asked a direct question, they don't mind being truthful and saying, "I do not know" rather than telling a lie.

It is ridiculous to lie to the Holy Spirit. He already knows the truth. When one makes false or misleading statements to other individuals, they should realize that in this age of technology, people can fact check you before you complete your lie. Therefore, it is wise to know when to speak and when to listen or keep silent.

"*Eat when the food is ready;*
speak when the time is right."
(Ethiopian proverb)

"*To everything there is a season, and a time*
to every purpose under the heaven."
(Ecclesiastes 3:1)

Read Ecclesiastes 3:1–8.

Comments:

Food tastes best if served and eaten at the appropriate time. Some foods are supposed to be served warm or hot, and other foods are best when cool or cold. In order to acquire the gratification, we wait until the food is ready to eat it. We do not delay and wait for a period of time because the quality and taste may change if the time is not right.

We should think on these same terms as we engage in conversations. We should only speak when the time is right. Speaking at inappropriate times leads to misunderstandings and problems. Wars have commenced because individuals spoke at the wrong time.

The first chapter of Ecclesiastes provides extensive narrative on times and seasons to do different things. If we follow the counsel of Solomon in the passages above, we readily conclude that there is a time and purpose for everything. We get poor results when we do things out of season or at the wrong time. Studying God's Word enhances our ability to discern the times and seasons.

Gabon Proverbs
—— and ——
Biblical Scriptures

*"Bad friends will prevent you from
having good friends."*
(Gabon proverb)

*"Be not deceived: Evil communications
corrupt good manners."*
(Proverbs 15:33)

*"Make no friendship with an angry man; and
with a furious man thou shalt not go: Lest thou
learn his ways, and set a snare to thy soul."*
(Proverbs 22:24–25)

*"Faithful are the wounds of a friend; but the
kisses of an enemy are deceitful."*
(Proverbs 27:6)

"Can two walk together, except they be agreed?"
(Amos 3:3)

Comments:

Read the comments in the section on Congolese proverbs under "The friends of our friends are our friends" (Congolese proverb). Also, in section on African proverbs, read comments under "Show me your friends, and I will show you your character" (African proverb).

Ganda Proverbs
—————— and ——————
Biblical Scriptures

"An ugly child of your own is more to you than a beautiful one belonging to your neighbor."
(Ganda proverb)

"Thou shalt not covet thy neighbour's house, thou shalt not covet thy neighbour's wife, nor his manservant, nor his maidservant, nor his ox, nor his ass, nor any thing that is thy neighbour's."
(Exodus 20:17)

"In everything give thanks: For this is the will of God in Christ Jesus concerning you."
(1 Thessalonians 5:18)

Read Psalm 127:3–5.

Comments:

We should be thankful for every gift that comes from God. In Psalm 127:3–5, we are told that children are an heritage from God. They are among the most precious gifts of all. They are a part of God and us. Psalm 127, verses 3–5, the narrative explains the ways they are precious and some of the ways they a blessing to us.

The reference in Exodus given above tells us we are not to covet anything that belongs to our neighbor. Everything He gave our neighbor is for our neighbor. Whether we realize it or not, everything He gives us is precious. Also, we should appreciate the beauty in all things created by God.

I do not know how others feel, but all of my children are gracious, precious, and beautiful blessings from God. The children of my neighbors are also precious. All of our children were awesomely and wonderfully made by God.

Let us be thankful for what God grants our neighbors. However, it should not be thought of as more beautiful or precious than what He has given us. Each gift, whether children or something else that God grants is uniquely fashioned and designed especially for the one to whom He gives it. As one songwriter expresses it, "What God Has for Me Is for Me!"

Additional comments can be found in the African proverbs section under "Children are the reward of life" (African proverb).

Ghanaian Proverbs
—————— and ——————
Biblical Scriptures

"You should not hoard your money and die of hunger."
(Ghanaian proverb)

"For the love of money is the root of all evil: which while some coveted after, they have erred from the faith, and pierced themselves through with many sorrows."
(1 Timothy 6:10)

Comments:

The above Scripture is discussed in various sections of this book. In each context, the implications may be slightly different, depending on the African proverb with which it is coupled. However, in every circumstance, it is "the love of money" that births the relative evil.

Can you imagine someone loving money so much that they will not purchase food to eat? Well, I recall a person who hoarded their money and ate out of a soup kitchen where the meals were free. She was a person who had survived the Great Depression. The concern was that she was very wealthy and hoarded her money, supposedly out of fear. One would think that if such a person managed to get rich after the Great Depression, he or she would be more secure. Instead, this person ate at the homeless shelter where others had far greater needs.

When used wisely, money is a great blessing to the individual and society. Imagine the quality of life for everyone if the five percent of people owning the mass of wealth would generously share it with the remaining ninety-five percent!

"Money is not the medicine against death."
(Ghanaian proverb)

*"And a woman having an issue of blood twelve
years, which had spent all her living upon physicians,
neither could be healed of any, came behind Him
and touched the border of His garment:*
And immediately her issue of blood stanched."
(Luke 8:43–44)

*"For the love of money is the root of all evil: which while
some coveted after, they have erred from the faith, and
pierced themselves through with many sorrows."*
(1 Timothy 6:10)

*"But Peter said unto him, thy money perish with
thee, because thou hast thought that the gift
of God may be purchased with money."*
(Acts 8:20)

Comments:

Money can buy a lot of things, but it cannot purchase life or health. This was evidenced by the woman who had the issue of blood. She spent all of her money trying to pay the doctors to make her well. They were not able to bring healing to her body, However, when she met Jesus, she concluded that faith in Jesus could do what all her money and the physicians were unable to accomplish. Faith in Jesus and just a touch of the border of His garment was all she needed to end a twelve-year long issue of blood.

In Acts 8:20, Peter informs an individual that the gift of God cannot be purchased with money. If one depends on money for healing or the gift of God, both the individual and his or her money will perish. One only needs to have faith. Additional information about faith can be found by reading the following Scriptures: Luke 17:5–6, Matthew 17:20, and Matthew 13:31–32.

God is still working miracles and doing what neither money nor physicians have ever been able to accomplish. I remember that over five decades ago my little sister suffered severe burns. The doctors did not expect her to survive and told my parents she would only live a few days. Thank God! The doctors did not have the last saying. A local preacher, a great man of God, Elder Keevie Lee Hooks came to the hospital and prayed for her. He talked the fire out of her, and fifty plus years later, she is alive, beautiful, and well. All of the glory and honor belongs to God, but thanks is also owed to the man of God who allowed himself to be used by the Master Physician."

Elder Hooks also prayed for my mother who was often hospitalized with asthma. After his prayer with her, I do not ever recall her being in the hospital for asthma again. This is not to suggest by any means that God does not use doctors. I am certain that if you read many of the available accounts throughout history, you will conclude the Master Physician, uses doctors to manifest some of His miracles. The key is to understand the finished work is not by the doctor's merits but by the awesome power of God!

"You become wise when you begin to run out of money."
(Ghanaian proverb)

Read the Parable of the Prodigal Son, Luke 15:11–32.

"Woe unto them that are wise in their own eyes, and prudent in their own sight!"
(Isaiah 5:21)

Read 1 Timothy 6:10, Proverbs 3:7, and Proverbs 26:12.

Comments:

The Parable of the Prodigal Son is an excellent example of one who became wise after he ran out of money. When he had an abundance of money, the Prodigal Son was wise in his own eyes. It is amazing how we can think we know everything when we have money or things are going well. However, when the money runs out and trouble prevails, it does not take long to recognize the errors of our ways.

The Prodigal Son was certain if he could change tradition and get his inheritance early, he would have it made on easy street. It did not work out as he thought. After he received the money from his inheritance, he soon wasted his finances on riotous living. When the money was depleted, he became hungry and had to work in a demeaning job. He came to his senses and remembered he had it much better before he requested his inheritance.

Upon realizing his sins, he decided to return home and ask for forgiveness. He was so full of remorse that he was willing to go back in a servant capacity. Thankfully, he had a loving father who welcomed him back and restored him as a son. Even greater, we have a loving Savior and Father in heaven who forgives us and imputes righteousness unto us. He restores us in loving fellowship with Him.

"If ten cents does not go out,
it does not bring in one thousand dollars."
(Ghanaian proverb)

Read the Parable of the Talents in Matthew 25:14–30

"Bring ye all the tithes into the storehouse, that there
may be meat in mine house, and prove me now
herewith, saith the Lord of Hosts, if I will not open you
the windows of heaven, and pour you out a blessing,
that there shall not be room enough to receive it."
(Malachi 3:10)

"Give, and it shall be given unto you;
good measure, pressed down, and shaken together,
and running over, shall men give into your bosom.
For with the same measure that ye mete withal
it shall be measured to you again."
(Luke 6:38)

"I have shewed you all things, how that so laboring
ye ought to support the weak, and to remember
the words of the Lord Jesus, how he said, it is
more blessed to give than to receive."
(Acts 20:35)

Comments:

In the Ghanaian proverb above, we are reminded that if you
want to increase wealth, you must begin by investing some of what
you already possess. Entrepreneurs desiring to start a new venture

must generate start-up capital. This is often called seed money. If you want a harvest, one of the first things you do is plant seeds.

The Bible references indicate methods that were utilized to effectively provide for the priesthood and worship facilities. In addition, provisions were made for the widows, orphans, and the needy. Only a small fraction of the increase of individuals was requested. When a multitude works together, it does not take a lot from any one person to acquire what is needed.

On a personal basis, if one desires to build wealth, with God's help and guidance, it is not difficult. His guidance can be found through prayer and studying the Word of God.

Note: Currently, I am in the process of compiling a book that will be called *Exponential Growth: The Doubling Effect.* For information on this project, please contact me at J. L. Bynum, 202 E. Church St., P.O. Box 119, Conetoe, NC 27819. You may also contact me by email at revjlb6@gmail.com.

This book will be a disciplined approach to wealth building by simplistic means. It is not a get-rich-quick scheme. The approach will require discipline, ingenuity, and work, work, and more work. If you have access to a computer, you can literally start with zero financial investment.

Your assistance would be greatly appreciated in its development. If you have money-saving tips, please share them with me. Also, if you have financial growth projects that are honest, moral, ethical, legitimate, and legal, that information would be welcome. Providing the information is useful in the furtherance of my project, if there are limited capital requirements, I would certainly be willing to invest in your ventures.

See Appendix: *Exponential Growth: The Doubling Effect.*

Proverbial Tree

*"A healthy person who begs for food is
an insult to a generous farmer."*
(Ghanaian proverb)

*"For even when we were with you,
this we commanded you, that if any would
not work, neither should he eat."*
(2 Thessalonians 3:10)

Comments:

In most societies and cultures, healthy individuals are expected to work. Provisions are generally made, without reservations, to assist those who are incapable of helping themselves. However, as Paul was reminding the church, according to their traditions, if a person was unwilling to work, neither should he or she eat. One of the reasons he was making these declarations was because false prophets and lovers of filthy lucre were arising. They were taking advantage of people and requesting that the people provide for their financial desires.

Guinean Proverbs
————— and —————
Biblical Scriptures

"Knowledge without wisdom is like water in the sand."
(Guinean proverb)

*"Happy is the man that findeth wisdom, and
the man that getteth understanding."*
(Proverbs 3:13)

*"The Lord by wisdom hath founded the earth;
by understanding hath He established the heavens."*
(Proverbs 3:19) Read Proverbs 3:13–20.

Comments:

In essence, knowledge alone is of little or no value. It is wasted if it is not accompanied by wisdom and understanding. If a person has knowledge about a given subject, but he has no wisdom and understanding regarding the practical application of what he has learned, it will not do him any good.

The narrative in Proverbs 3:13–20, provides detailed accounts of knowledge, wisdom, and understanding. It is imperative that one knows that wisdom comes from God.

Reflections:

My older brother, Robert, spent a lot of time teaching me many things about auto mechanics. I learned most of the parts of the motor, but I was at a lost when it came time to apply what I had learned. It definitely was not because he did not take time to teach me well. Patiently, he used visuals, hands-on experience, labeling, and modeling. However, I had serious difficulties with interest. Therefore, for the most part, the knowledge he imparted drained from me as rapidly as water soaking through sand.

Kenyan Proverbs

—————— and ——————

Biblical Scriptures

"Traveling is learning."
(Kenyan proverb)

Read Numbers 13.

Comments:

In the discourse in Numbers 13, God instructs Moses to have twelve men to travel to Canaan. Their specific purpose for the journey is to spy out the land. During their travels, their goal is to learn things, such as the population, the strength of the people, the quality of the land, types of cities and housing, and the produce.

They completed their travels (spying) after forty days and brought back a report of what they learned. In addition to the verbal report, they came back with grapes, pomegranates, and figs as evidence or proof of what they learned. The report was confirmation what God had promised, "a land flowing with milk and honey." However, as a result of unbelief and fear, many of them never made it to this promised land.

Reflections:

As I read the above Kenyan proverb, I took a retrospective look at certain aspects of my travel experiences from childhood to the present. By the time I was in the sixth grade, I had attended eight different schools. I excelled academically in all of my classes but had difficulty making and keeping friends. Nevertheless, the constant moving provided rich opportunities for learning experiences and cultural growth and development.

One of my most enlightening trips was when I was in the eighth grade. Our field trip for that year was a trip to the North Carolina State Fair. Prior to that time, I had never been to a county fair, circus, or carnival. When we arrived at the fair in Raleigh, North Carolina, I remained in the company of a few friends who were apparently as naïve as myself. I thought the fair consisted of only the games and the rides.

Upon returning to school, we had class discussions about our experiences at the fair. I was amazed when others showed brochures, post cards, gifts, and souvenirs from various exhibits. I was shocked to learn that the pictures of large buildings like Dorton Arena and the Scott Building were part of the fair. I had not been aware that any of the agricultural and craft exhibits existed.

There is an African proverb that says, "The fool speaks; the wise man listens." I did not want to appear to be a fool that day, so I did a lot of listening (and learning). I also promised myself I would travel extensively in the future and capitalize on the total travel experience.

Later in life, as an adult, I made it a priority to take my children on numerous trips. Almost every year after the first child was able to walk, we visited the North Carolina State Fair. They were privileged to enjoy the rides, games, and great food. In addition, I ascertained they visited most of the exhibits, crafts, and some of the appropriate shows.

Although we were a low-income family, we were privileged to take many trips. We visited every East Coast state from Florida to New York. We always stopped at the visitors' centers at state lines. We collected post cards, brochures, and maps at every opportunity. My wife also loved to stop by the roadside and collect rocks and flowers for her collection.

We also visited other states, including Louisiana, Tennessee, and Kentucky. Our favorite family trips were to Disney World (numerous times) and a cruise to the Bahamas. My most exhilarating traveling excursions, without the joys of family, were to Israel, Greece, Canada, Ghana, Nigeria, Ethiopia, and several other African countries.

As a child, my traveling experiences were primarily the dreams associated with the books I read and pictures I had seen. When I was finally able to visit some of those places, I realized how much was missed by not actually experiencing the people, lands, cultures, and attractions.

In conclusion, if a picture is worth a thousand words, then actual travel and cultural experiences must be worth a million words. Neither words nor pictures are able to capture what you learn and experience real time through the use of your sensory skills.

Malagasy Proverbs
—————— and ——————
Biblical Scriptures

"Good words are food, bad words poison."
(Malagasy proverb)

"Thy words were found, and I did eat them; and thy word was unto me the joy and rejoicing of mine heart: For I am called by thy name, O Lord God of hosts."
(Jeremiah 15:16)

"But he answered and said, it is written, man shall not live by bread alone, but by every word that proceedeth out of the mouth of God."
(Matthew 4:4)

"But the tongue can no man tame; it is an unruly evil, full of deadly poison."
(James 3:8)

Read James 3:8–10.

*"Let no corrupt communication proceed out of your
mouth, but that which is good to the use for edifying,
that it may minister grace unto the hearers. And grieve
not the Holy Spirit of God, whereby ye are sealed
unto the day of redemption. Let all bitterness, and
wrath, and anger, and clamour, and evil speaking, be
put away from you, with all malice: And be ye kind
one to another, tenderhearted, forgiving one another,
even as God for Christ's sake hath forgiven you."*
(Ephesians 4:29–32)

Comments:

The divine voice of God spoke good words, and the beauty and splendor of all that we enjoy was created. His divine voice spoke, and everything that was made, God made it. He also made man in His likeness and image. God spoke, put man in a deep sleep, performed a divine operation, took a rib from man's side, and created woman. Genesis, chapters 1 and 2 tell of these wonderful works of God. His nourishing words provided everything man would need to sustain.

After God's creation, the deceitful, bad words of the enemy, Satan, came through the serpent and tried to poison or destroy man (Genesis 3:1–13). From that time forth, there are accounts throughout the Bible demonstrating how Satan, through bad words, cunning devices, and deceit, tries to steal, kill, and destroy. Satan, like poison, tries to destroy. One of the most read accounts of Satan's destructiveness is in the book of Job. It is a story of how Satan wants to challenge the integrity of a servant of God. In essence, the deceiver is attempting to challenge God Himself.

There are narratives throughout the Bible that illustrate how good words are like food (especially the Word of God). A good Bible reference or internet search will provide accounts of hundreds of healings and other miracles as a result of good words from God and man. In two New Testament accounts, Jesus multiplies a few fish and a small amount of bread and feeds thousands (Luke 9:10–17 and Matthew 15:32–39). Unfortunately, but truthfully, you will also find many references of bad words from Satan (the devil or enemy) and some men who conduct acts as destructive and deadly as poison. Narratives of Satan using bad words in the temptation of Jesus are found in Mark 1, beginning at verse twelve and Luke 4, starting at verse eleven.

Reflections:

The phrase "Sticks and stones may break my bones, but names (or words) can never hurt me" was used often during my childhood. It was a response used when individuals called us names or spoke harmful words to hurt us. We often gave the response in order to avoid trouble and imply that words or names caused no physical pain. It may have aided in the avoidance of physical confrontation, but emotionally, it was painful and poisonous to be bullied by name calling and hurtful words.

Thankfully, there were also people who spoke good words or kind, motivational words. These words were soothing and like food and medicine, helped to decrease or eliminate the pain. Also, the Bible or Word of God, provides comforting, inspirational, nourishing, and soothing words that are like a healing balm and nutrition for the soul.

The love of God should inspire us to refrain from using bad or corrupt words. We should endeavor to speak good, fruitful words that will lead to eternal life and fellowship with God and man. One of the best ways to ensure we are speaking words that are like food is to study the Holy Bible. If we emulate the words, actions, and deeds of Jesus, we are certain to be on the right pathway. Further, yield your life totally to Christ and accept Him as Lord and Savior.

Moroccan Proverbs
— and —
Biblical Scriptures

"Instruction in youth is like engraving in stone."
(Moroccan proverb)

"Train up a child in the way he should go, and when he is old, he will not depart from it."
(Proverbs 22:6)

"He that spareth his rod hateth his son: But he that loveth him chasteneth him betimes."
(Proverbs 13:24)

Comments:

When one engraves in stone, the expectation is that the engraving will stand the test of time, storms, and other elements. If you engrave in wood, in a few years, the wood may decay, and the engraving is lost. Other mediums, such as paper, are even less durable.

Instruction in youth is expected to last throughout the life of the individual. When the individual ages, it is likely that he or she will remember instructions they received in youth. That is why it is so important to teach children when they are young.

A great illustration of the importance of instruction in youth is the Parable of the Prodigal Son. Imagine the consequences if he had not been instructed in youth. He was able to realize the errors of his ways because he had been instructed by his father. If he had not received previous instruction and experiences, he would not have had knowledge of how much better things could be back at home. Therefore, he would have probably continued living beneath his privileges.

It is crucial that young people be provided with good instruction. As they mature, they are confronted with so many challenges in life. Good instruction will help when they reach those situations in life that require them to make difficult choices. It is a blessing for our children to know that there are choices better than drugs, sexual immorality, riotous living, and other evils of life. Make sure young people have received proper instruction so that when the time comes that they need to choose between good and evil, they can say, "I will arise and go back home where I know things are better."

Note: See comments in section on African proverbs: "It takes a village to raise a child" (African proverb).

Moroccan Proverbs and Biblical Scriptures

ﻌﯨﻌﻊ

Three things cause sorrow to flee: water,
green trees, and a beautiful face."
(Moroccan proverb)

"A merry heart doeth good like a medicine:
But a broken spirit drieth the bones."
(Proverbs 17:22)

"And Sarah said, God hath made me to laugh,
so that all that hear will laugh with me."
(Genesis 21:6)

"A time to weep, and a time to laugh; a
time mourn, and a time to dance;"
(Ecclesiastes 3:4)

Read Ecclesiastes 3:1–8.

Read John 16:16–24, Revelation 2:10–11, and
Revelation 21:1–4.

"Honour and majesty are before Him: strength
and beauty are in His sanctuary."
(Psalm 96:6)

Comments:

When I think of the three things in the Moroccan proverb that cause sorrow to flee, the beauty and splendor of all that God has created immediately comes to mind. Whenever troubles, trials, tribulations, sorrows, or any disturbing situations or circumstances come my way, I try to reflect on the majesty and goodness of God. It diminishes or eliminates sorrow. Appreciating the beauty of God's handiwork brings smiles and joy.

If one simply looks at the water, trees, flowers, birds, creatures, and especially mankind, sorrow has to flee. When our hearts are full of gratitude, it is difficult to focus on sorrows.

Reflections:

One of my favorite greetings and benedictions to family, friends, and even enemies is "It is a beautiful day in the kingdom of God. Enjoy the beauty and splendor of all that God has created and have some fun!" Recently, one of my friends, Lynette Hooks, told me how the expression has changed the way she sees a number of things. She shared that after meditating and reflecting on what I had said, she began to see sunrises, sunsets, trees, and all of creation differently. She began to literally see beauty in all of God's creation. Imagine the newfound joy of seeing beauty in all things around you. Imagine the smiles on the faces of others as they look on your countenance! Imagine the joy, peace, and happiness of experiencing the love of God as you are grateful for all that He has done and is continually doing!

"There is no beauty but the beauty of action."
(Moroccan proverb)

*"And how shall they preach, except they be
sent? As it is written, how beautiful are the feet
of them that preach the gospel of peace,
and bring glad tidings of good things!"*
(Romans 15:16)

Read Isaiah 52:7–10.

Comments:

There is a special beauty in positive actions. I love the thoughts of enjoying the beauty and splendor of all that God has created. Reading about the awesomeness, of God, His beautiful creations, His majesty, His love, kindness, peace, and joy touch my heart. However, the beauty expands when I am able to engage in activities that allow me to experience that beauty.

Some of the most beautiful people, places, and things that I have been exposed to are those I was privileged to see in person. Also, I was able to actively engage in communication, events, and/or activities. Beauty is often appreciated through singing, dancing, games, listening to music, and many activities that allow engagement and participation.

There is spiritual beauty in allowing God to use you to His glory. One of the greatest expressions of beauty is the preaching of the gospel.

Paul, in his epistle to the Romans, expresses the beauty of preaching the gospel and bringing glad tidings of good things. There is also beauty in witnessing positive responses to the preaching as individuals accept salvation through Jesus Christ. In addition, there is great beauty in experiencing the love, joy, and peace of knowing Christ and being in fellowship with Him. When you put your faith and trust in Christ, there is beauty that surpasses all understanding. That beauty will change your total countenance and outlook on life. It will be like a brand new you!"

Nigerian Proverbs
— and —
Biblical Scriptures

"Fine words do not produce food."
(Nigerian proverb)

"Beauty is not sold and eaten."
(Nigerian proverb)

*"For even when we were with you,
this we commanded you, that if any would
not work, neither should he eat."*
(2 Thessalonians 3:10)

Comments:

In both of the above Nigerian proverbs, the reader is reminded that some things, such as beauty and fine words or speech do not put food on the table. Regardless of which society or nation one lives in, if he or she has health and strength, the person is expected to work to provide for their sustenance.

How pathetic it would be if your beauty or fine words was the way you received food! What would happen when the beauty fades or the speech slurs?

I realize that in a few situations, people have occupations such as motivational speakers. Yet, if the persons wants to be paid, he has to work, study, and present in an acceptable manner. Otherwise, he will not be able to continue making presentations.

If you plan to get your funds from beauty contests, they are limited. Also, know that there are other beautiful people. Further, think of what happens when the wrinkles come, the steps shorten, the hump takes over the back, and the beauty is gone.

In 2 Thessalonians, Paul reminded the church of the training and traditions of the ages. If you are able, you should work. Don't expect others to take care of you. If you are unable to work, however, do not be dismayed. When you have done all that you can do, then trust God's love and providence to meet your needs. Even with Paul's teachings, provisions were made for widows, orphans, the poor, and others who were not able to work.

Nigerian Proverbs and Biblical Scriptures

*"The wise create proverbs for fools to learn,
not to repeat."*
(Nigerian proverb)

**Read Proverbs 1 and then all of Proverbs and
Ecclesiastes. In addition, proverbs, maxims, and wisdom
sayings can be found throughout the Bible. They will
further amplify the use and significance
of proverbs.**

Comments:

You can repeat proverbs, maxims, and wisdom sayings throughout the day! Yet, if you do not learn them and apply them to life's situations and circumstances, they will be of little or no value. One should learn them to the point that implementation of the wisdom garnered from them is automatically utilized daily. They were created to make life simpler. If practically applied, they are basic enough so even a fool should be able to find his way.

"Wealth diminishes with usage;
learning increases with use."
(Nigerian proverb)

"For the Lord giveth wisdom: out of his mouth
cometh knowledge and understanding."
(Proverbs 2:6)

"A wise man will hear, and will increase learning; and
a man of understanding shall attain unto wise counsels:
To understand a proverb, and the interpretation;the
words of the wise, and their dark sayings."
(Proverbs:1:5–6)

"Give instruction to a wise man, and he will be yet wiser:
teach a just man, and he will increase in learning."
(Proverbs 9:9)

Comments:

There is a Cameroon proverb that says, "Knowledge is better than riches." Apparently, the creator of this proverb was aware that riches and wealth diminish as you use them. Further, wealth and riches will decay and/or decrease in value over a period of time. Thieves may break in and take away all of your belongings. According to the Scriptures, learning increases. As learning is used and the learner accepts counsel and teaching, he becomes wiser. If he makes practical application of the wisdom, knowledge, and understanding he receives from God, they will be the tools that will allow him to obtain the possessions he needs.

Senegalese Proverbs
———— and ————
Biblical Scriptures

"There can be no peace without understanding."
(Senegalese proverb)

"And the peace of God, which passeth all understanding,
shall keep your hearts and minds through Christ Jesus.
Finally, brethren, whatsoever things are true, whatsoever
things are honest, whatsoever things are just, whatsoever
things are pure, whatsoever things are lovely, whatsoever
things are of good report; if there be any virtue, and if
there be any praise, think on these things. Those things,
which ye have both learned, and received, and heard, and
seen in me, do: And the God of peace shall be with you."
(Philippians 4:7–9)

"Therefore being justified by faith, we have peace
with God through our Lord Jesus Christ: by whom
also we have access by faith into this grace wherein
we stand, and rejoice in hope of the glory of God."
(Romans 5:1–2)

Proverbial Tree

Read Romans 5:1–4.

Comments:

Tranquility can only be achieved if one knows or understands what is necessary for him to feel at peace. Every person is unique. It is impossible to determine what is peaceful for you based on what another considers to be tranquil. For example, I come from a large family and love what I call "good noise." The noise must be free from envy, strife, pain or suffering, or similar elements. When noise is accompanied by laughter, singing, dancing, games, and fun, I love it! On the other hand, some of my children have difficulty tolerating noise. When my grandchildren are running around having a good time, I often hear my children saying, "Please sit down for a little while and let me have some peace and quiet." I wonder if my children recall how noisy they were in their youth!

When we think of peace as the absence of war, understanding must also be present to achieve tranquility. You will not be able to avoid conflict if you are not aware of the elements that cause confusion. There must be mutual respect and acceptance of the rights and privileges of others. Sometimes, in order to keep peace, it is necessary to ascertain that your rights do not infringe on the rights of others. In addition, there are times when it is essential that each party is willing to compromise.

Guidelines, laws, legal codes, and religious codes have been established in most places. These guidelines, laws, and codes are put in place to help maintain peace. If you want to understand them, start by reading and learning about them. Whether it is another country, or another individual, you will not know if you are infringing on the rights of others if you have no knowledge of those rights. My favorite texts for the novice and the well-educated are the Holy Bible and the United States Constitution. Both of these documents are complex, so do not be dismayed that you will not be able to comprehend much of the literature in your initial readings.

Finally, if you want to be at peace with others, you need to begin by being at peace with yourself. In order to do so, you should search yourself within and without, and know what you believe. You must know what you accept as your moral standards and codes of conduct. For me, that meant setting standards for every aspect of my life. In order to accomplish these goals, I had to strive to be at peace with myself, God, family, and my fellow man.

Somalian Proverbs

——————— and ———————

Biblical Scriptures

*"If you can't resolve your problems in
peace, you can't solve war."*
(Somalian proverb)

**Read the Scriptures in the previous section,
"Senegalese Proverbs and Biblical Scriptures."**

Comments:

Read the comments in the previous section, "Senegalese Proverbs and Biblical Scriptures." Wars usually start as a result of confusion and misunderstandings. There is less confusion, conflict, and chaos during times of tranquility. If people cannot sit down and talk through their problems during those times, they certainly cannot when they are fighting.

When the battle is over, the problem remains. In most cases, additional problems and conflicts occur. The battle usually ends because one party was more powerful, out maneuvered, or conquered the other. The loser may simply wait for a more opportune time to settle the matter. For that reason, many countries have been in multiple conflicts with each other for centuries.

By the same token, there are individuals who are unforgiving. They will hold grudges for generations. Have you ever heard (or heard of) individuals who say, "I will get you back if it is the last thing I do!" Problems can never be resolved under such circumstances.

"Poverty is slavery."
(Somalian proverb)

"The rich ruleth over the poor,
and the borrower is servant to the lender."
(Proverbs 22:7)

"If the Son therefore shall make you
free, ye shall be free indeed."
(John 8:36)

Read Jeremiah 29:1–2. Then read all of Jeremiah 29.

Comments:

More than four centuries later, neither African Americans, Native Americans, nor people of color are free. The great documents such as the Emancipation Proclamation of 1863, the 13th Amendment of 1865, the Civil Rights Acts of 1964 and 1968, or other documents have not extended freedom to all citizens. Each of the documents have fallen short in provision of equality and freedom. Systematically, a portion of the Caucasian majority in the United States of America have found ways of maintaining oppression of its people of color.

Some would argue that this cannot be true because America has had its first African American president. Further, they would argue that a number of people of color and Native Americans have held high offices in the political arena. However, I would counter that it does not end the poverty and social, economic, political, and religious injustices in America.

One may ask, "how can we escape from slavery?" Although the conditions were different in Jeremiah 29, I believe we can garner great wisdom by examining the narrative. It is a letter, penned by Jeremiah the prophet, to people of Israel who had been carried away as captives to Babylon. Jeremiah's prophecy was mandated by God to His people of Israel.

I am confident that God can and will do the same for me that He has done for others. I believe "All Scripture is given by inspiration of God, and is profitable for doctrine, for reproof, for correction, for instruction in righteousness: That the man of God may be perfect, thoroughly furnished unto all good works" (2 Timothy 3:16–17). So as I examine the prophecy of Jeremiah in Jeremiah 29, I believe the words can be profitable today. There are seven elements of the prophecy that I believe can help us escape from slavery (or poverty). First, build houses and live in them (Jeremiah 29:5). Second, plant gardens and eat their fruit (Jeremiah 29:5). Third, multiply and reproduce. Multiply and increase! Don't diminish! (Jeremiah 29:6). Fourth, seek peace and pray for it (Jeremiah 29:7). Fifth, trust God and have faith (Jeremiah 29:11). Sixth, call upon God and pray (Jeremiah 29:12). Seventh, seek God and search for Him with all your heart and you will find Him (Jeremiah 29:13–14).

It is easy when things are not going well to lose hope and give up. However, as you will note, Jeremiah gave prophetic instructions (from God) to be productive and proactive even during dismal times. Trust and believe that God has a plan for us. Be as productive as possible because you may be setting yourself up for a blessing. How many times have you recognized that in some situations and circumstances when others were trying to take advantage of you, you received the greater blessing? Time and time again, you will find examples in the Word of God and in life that when others commit evil deeds, God will work it out for our good.

"Wisdom does not come overnight."
(Somalian proverb)

"Hear, ye children, the instruction of a father, and attend to know understanding."
(Proverbs 4:1)

"For the Lord giveth wisdom: out of His mouth cometh knowledge and understanding."
(Proverbs 2:6).

Read Proverbs 2:6–8.

"The fear of the Lord is the beginning of knowledge:
but fools despise wisdom and instruction."
(Proverbs 1:7)

"I have written unto you, fathers, because ye
have known Him that is from the beginning.
I have written unto you, young men, because ye
are strong, and the Word of God abideth in you,
and ye have overcome the wicked one."
(1 John 2:14)

**Also, read 1 John 2:13–15. Read Proverbs 4:5–9,
Proverbs 8, Psalm 111:10, and Ecclesiastes 8.**

Comments:

Most theologians agree that Solomon, son of King David, was the wisest man ever known. He did not get his wisdom overnight, nor was he born with it. He requested wisdom from God and God granted it to him. As you search the Scriptures above, you will recognize that wisdom comes from God.

Think of the training or education you have received in life. Were you able to apply everything you learned soon after you learned it? I do not know how things worked out for you, but I did not have the wisdom to practically apply much of what I learned until later. Imagine a physician just getting out of medical school. He has completed his internship but has still not had experience in many areas. However, as he or she practices medicine, wisdom and additional knowledge comes with time. I say practice because regardless to the amount of training, I am a firm believer that the wisdom comes from God.

In Proverbs 1:7, we are reminded that *"The fear of the Lord is the beginning of knowledge ... "* In Psalm 111:10, it is recorded with a slight variation and the word "knowledge" is changed to wisdom. Our knowledge and wisdom begins when we become aware of the truths of God. As we learn more about the omnipotence, omnipresence, and omniscience of God, our wisdom increases. Sometimes our learning comes from divine impartation or inspiration of the Holy Spirit. Other times, He will give us wisdom through experiences and/or dreams.

As a child, I often heard a song that said, "Every day with Jesus is sweeter than the day before." The more I learn about God, the more I realize the truth of the song. For almost twelve years, I have had zero physical vision. Many people find it difficult to believe, but when I tell others that I am currently at one of the happiest and most joyous points in my life, I am serious. God is so amazing! Since I accepted Christ into my life at age fifteen, I have been assured of the power and goodness of God. However, now I can truthfully say, "I know that I know that I know that I know God." He is so amazing!

Somalian Proverbs and Biblical Scriptures

"One cannot count on riches."
(Somalian proverb)

*"Trust not in oppression, and become not vain in robbery:
If riches increase, set not your heart upon them."*
(Psalm 62:10)

*"A good name is rather to be chosen than great riches,
and loving favour rather than silver and gold."*
(Proverbs 22:1)

Comments:

Money can buy a lot of things. Yet, it is not something you can count upon. If you are hungry, all the money in the world would be worthless if there is a famine and no food to be purchased. Money cannot buy love, health, or life. God's grace, mercy, redemption, the breath of life, and divine favor are not things or objects that can be bought and sold.

Riches will fade away and perish. If used, wealth will decrease as you use it. If you don't use it, it is valueless. God's love is everlasting and since He promised to always be with us, we can trust Him at His Word.

The example of the woman who had the issue of blood for twelve years explains further about reasons we should trust God rather than riches. Read about this miraculous account in three of the Gospels: Matthew 9:20–22, Mark 5:25–34, and Luke 8:43–48.

Read the comments under the Ghanaian proverb "Money is not the medicine against death."

Proverbial Tree

ʊ§ʔʊ

"One shares food, not words."
(Somalian proverb)

"If thine enemy be hungry, give him bread to eat; and if he be thirsty, give him water to drink: For thou shalt heap coals of fire upon his head, and the Lord shall reward thee."
(Proverbs 25:21–22)

"Therefore if thine enemy hunger, feed him; if he thirst, give him drink: For in so doing thou shalt heap coals of fire on his head. Be not overcome of evil, but overcome evil with good."
(Romans 12:20–21).

Read Isaiah 58:6–12.

"He that hath a bountiful eye shall be blessed; for he giveth of his bread to the poor."
(Proverbs 22:9)

"He that giveth unto the poor shall not lack: but he that hideth his eyes shall have many a curse."
(Proverbs 28:27)

Read Matthew 14:13–21.

Comments:

Research the longest words in English, Spanish, French, Swahili, and a few other languages. More than likely, you found some fairly long words with both vowels and consonants. Now, look up the longest words in the same languages that have only vowels or consonants. Check out each word carefully. How many of the words are of value to you if you are hungry? Smile!

When individuals are hungry, your words do not provide nourishment to them. If I am hungry, I do not care to hear of all the delicious meals that are available. I want to eat! It does not help to share how to get food in the distant future. If the person is hungry, feed him or her. If they are thirsty, go ahead and give them something to drink.

In the miraculous feeding of about five thousand, excluding women and children, Jesus shared words, but he also saw that the multitude was fed. His compassion went beyond their spiritual needs and included their physical needs. The disciples suggested that the multitude return to neighboring locations where they could get food. However, Jesus knew they were hungry and faint. He instructed the disciples to sit the multitude down and feed them. With His miraculous power, He took five loaves and fed the multitude.

We are also instructed to feed the hungry. It does not matter that we may have limited resources. When we share, Jesus will multiply our little, and it becomes much.

Read the comments under the following proverbs: "If relatives help each other, what evil can hurt them?" (African proverb).

"Beautiful words don't put porridge in the pot" (Botswana proverb).

"Fine words do not produce food" (Nigerian proverb).

Sudanese Proverbs
———— and ————
Biblical Scriptures

"A large chair does not make a king."
(Sudanese proverb)

"In the multitude of people is the king's honour: But in the want of people is the destruction of the prince."
(Proverbs 14:28)

"The king's heart is in the hand of the Lord, as the rivers of water: He turneth it whithersoever He will."
(Proverbs 21:1)

Read Romans 13. Pay particular attention to verses one through four. Also, read Revelation 1:6.

Comments:

It is so good to know neither large chairs, fine clothes, luxury cars, grandiose houses nor any tangible thing make kings, presidents, or leaders. Furthermore, their title does not make them a leader. Since wisdom, knowledge, and understanding come from God, as the Scriptures inform us, kings are turned, directed, or guided by the Lord. I realize in a democracy we vote for leaders, but as Jesus told Pilate, they would have no power at all except God gave it to them.

I am reminded that my uncle and former pastor, Elder William Ruffin Hyman, often reminded the congregation that "Satan can do no more than what my Father pleases." Well, I would add to that, neither can man. Regardless of who is in the White House (or any other place for leadership), God is still on the throne!

Reflections:

As I was writing, I began to reflect on the presidency of the current president of the United States of America, Donald Trump. Neither the White House, presidential title, nor anything else has been able to make him a leader. Instead of trying to bring about unity, he is constantly causing divisions. Before the end of his third year in office, he had been impeached by the House of Representatives. Also, through fact checks, it has been found that before completing three years in office, he had already told over sixteen hundred lies.

One of the most difficult things to comprehend about Trump's presidency is that he seems to share his leadership with the president of Russia, Vladimir Putin. In many cases, he has accepted Putin's word over the United States intelligence officials and the Federal Bureau of Investigations.

President Trump also blames others for his shortcomings. He blames former presidents, leaders of other countries, and even former political opponents. He seems to be obsessed with the successes of the forty-fourth president, Barak Obama. He has attempted to dismantle or demolish everything he could that led to his popularity as president. Instead of using his time wisely and seeking the advice of wise counselors, he seems to attach himself to the most corrupt people he can locate.

My recommendation to people like Donald Trump would be to understand that you never make yourself look good by trying to make someone else look bad. In addition, review the following African proverb: "If you close your eyes to facts you will learn by accident." Also, review the Ashanti proverb: "When a king has good counsellors, his reign is peaceful" (Ashanti proverb). Finally, read the Scriptures and comments that accompany the proverbs.

Swahili Proverbs

——————— and ———————

Biblical Scriptures

"Unity is strength; division is weakness."
(Swahili proverb)

"And if a house be divided against itself, that house cannot stand."
(Mark 3:25)

Read Psalm 133.

Comments:

Review the following African Proverbs and the Scriptures and the comments that accompany each of them.

"If you want to go quickly, go alone; if you want to go far, go together."

"If relatives help each other, what evil can hurt them?" Now, review the following Bondei proverb: "Sticks in a bundle are unbreakable." Read the Scriptures and comments that accompany it.

Reflections:

Have you ever been a participant in a group project with individuals who failed to share in the work? I recall a graduate school project requiring a presentation by a group of four individuals. Three of the individuals agreed on the theme for the presentation. The fourth person wanted to do something different. The one who wanted to do something different sabotaged the project by taking up seventy-five percent of the presentation time. Most of the material she presented was read without much passion. The remaining three presenters only had about thirty minutes to present. Therefore, much of the relevant material, as well as visual aids and movie clips had to be omitted. From my perspective, it was a disaster! After the professor cited the failure of full group participation, lack of professionalism, and missing facts, the grade she awarded us was a B. It was evident that we were not united. Although three were in agreement, division by one made it appear that our work was not coordinated.

There were also times when as many as ten people were supposed to share the workload. Some of those times only half the individuals participated. I recall a specific presentation for senior seminar. Everybody was supposed to write an individual paper on different courses and experiences during matriculation through graduate school. Two students had the responsibility of reviewing each of the individual papers and complete the final presentation. One of the individual papers was not turned in to the final writer until the due date. I intentionally used the term "final writer" because the writer called in about three days before due date and could not participate. A third person got angry because his schedule was different and refused to participate. However, no one deliberately worked to sabotage the project. Our final grade was an A. Naturally, everyone was pleased and took full credit for the work.

One day, I asked a friend, Evangelist Gloria Harris, about her greatest experiences with people working together in unity. Her favorite experiences were when she was in cosmetology school and barber school. She was passionate about both, but stated the greater experience was in barber school. She attended cosmetology school first. She liked the way everyone worked together to reach their educational and vocational goals.

After receiving her certification in cosmetology, Gloria enrolled as a student at Harris Barber College. Initially, she was the only female student in her barber school class. A number of people had tried to discourage her from attending barber school. However, she said it was something she began to enjoy when her dad would let her shave him. Gloria was only ten years old the first time she shaved her dad. She said it meant a lot to her that he trusted her that much. In addition, she enjoyed it.

When she was in barber school, she said at first it was not what she expected. As she began to learn, it was like a family.

Everybody worked well together and supported each other. The instructor worked diligently to ascertain they were all masters of their trade. Barber school was a lot of fun! She soon realized that was her forte. It was an exhilarating experience throughout training. The fun and love for the work continued after graduation when she became a licensed barber.

Another good memory of individuals working together in unity was when our church had financial difficulties and worked together to complete a new building project. We were a small congregation, but when most of the congregation united, with hard work, we reached our goal. It is a joy each time I visit that church and recall how young and old worked together. Through our united efforts and the favor of God, we now have a beautiful sanctuary which we trust will be a blessing for generations. We are still working together and having great times on our spiritual journey.

Proverbial Tree

"To run is not necessarily to arrive."
(Swahili proverb)

*"I returned, and saw under the sun, that the
race is not to the swift, nor the battle to the
strong, neither yet bread to the wise,
nor yet riches to men of understanding,
nor yet favour to men of skill;
but time and chance happeneth to them all."*
(Ecclesiastes 9:11)

*"But he that shall endure unto the end,
the same shall be saved."*
(Matthew 24:13)

*"Know ye not that they which run in a race run all, but
one receiveth the prize? So run, that ye may obtain."*
(1 Corinthians 9:24)

*"For I am now ready to be offered, and the time of my
departure is at hand. I have fought a good fight,
I have finished my course, I have kept the faith:
Henceforth there is laid up for me a crown of
righteousness, which the Lord, the righteous judge,
shall give me at that day: And not to me only,
but unto all them also that love his appearing."*
(2 Timothy 4:6–8)

Comments:

There is not a Scripture that says, "The race is not given to the swift, nor to the strong, but to him that endureth to the end." This saying is a combination of two Scriptures. A variation of this saying is found in a number of songs.

Have you ever watched athletes who started races at top speeds? Often, they get a good lead, but then run out of stamina. Then others who kept a steady pace easily pass by them. Sometimes, the one who starts out so fast is not able to complete the race. Many of the onlookers are surprised when that one they thought started out so slow is the first to cross the finish line.

Some competitions consist of multiple races. The winners are those who have the highest accumulation of points at the end of the final race. Small prizes are awarded at the end of each of the races leading up to the final. However, the grand prize goes to the person with the highest number of points.

In still other races, such as marathons, everyone strives for the higher prize or first place. Yet everyone who crosses the finish line is a winner. This race reminds me of the race of life or the spiritual race. If we run the Christian life in faith, all we have to do is endure until the end. Some may run faster than others, but that will not keep the slower individuals from getting their rewards and eternal life. At the end of life's journey, we will all be winners and receive the crown of eternal life. Our rewards may be different, but what greater prize than eternal life with everlasting joy, peace, and happiness!

Tanzanian Proverbs
—————— and ——————
Biblical Scriptures

"To be without a friend is to be poor indeed."
(Tanzanian proverb)

"Two are better than one; because they have a good reward for their labour. For if they fall, the one will lift up his fellow: But woe to him that is alone when he falleth; for he hath not another to help him up."
(Ecclesiastes 4:9–10)

Comments:

Read the Scriptures and comments that accompany the following two proverbs which appear in the section on African proverbs.

"If you want to go quickly, go alone; if you want to go far, go together" (African proverb).

"Hold a true friend with both hands" (African proverb). Have you ever heard the phrase "No man is an island?" It is a reminder that unlike an island, no man can make it alone. We all need each other. It is even better, however, to have friends. Friends will be there when you need them. Friends will share and sacrifice to ascertain that the needs of other friends are met. The needs are not always financial. There are times we will need the rich resources of our friends' love, moral, and spiritual support.

"Make some money, but don't let money make you."
(Tanzanian proverb)

"For the love of money is the root of all evil: which while some coveted after, they have erred from the faith, and pierced themselves through with many sorrows."
(1 Timothy 6:10)

Comments:

Years ago, probably sixty years or more, there was gospel group called Bill Moss and the Celestials. One of their songs was called "A Satisfied Mind." Both the music and lyrics were beautiful. You can probably listen to it by title and author at www.youtube.com.

The storyline is about a man's limited resources. He mentions the things he had to do without at times. After singing about what he doesn't have, the verses end with "As long as I've got Jesus, I've got a satisfied mind." At one point, he mentions not having any money. There are not a lot of people who can claim satisfaction when they are broke. But if you really know your source, it is not as bad.

I do not think one will find anywhere that it is written, "Money is evil." It is the love of money that causes evil deeds. We all need finances to take care of our needs. However, we should not get to the point that we will do anything to possess it. In addition, money should never possess us.

Even young children recognize the changes in the personalities of some people when they get a few extra dollars. I remember a jingle that said something in the order of "people act kind of funny when they get a little money!" Some of your so-called friends will walk away when they have more money than you. At that point, I believe they are allowing the money to make them. If that is the case, their money may increase, but their character diminishes.

Go back to the sections of the following proverbs and read the Scriptures and comments that accompany them:

"Greed loses what it has gained" (African proverb).

"Money is sharper than the sword" (Ashanti proverb).

"You should not hoard your money and die of hunger" (Ghanaian proverb).

Proverbial Tree

"Many hands make light work."
(Tanzanian proverb)

"Two ants do not fail to pull one grasshopper."
(Tanzanian proverb)

"Sticks in a bundle are unbreakable."
(Tanzanian proverb)

*"And if a house be divided against
itself, that house cannot stand."*
(Mark 3:25)

Read Psalm 133 and Ecclesiastes 4:9–12.

Comments:

Study the Scriptures and comments that accompany the following proverbs in their respective sections:

"If you want to go quickly, go alone; if you want to go far, go together" (African proverb).

"If relatives help each other, what evil can hurt them?" (African proverb).

"Unity is strength; division is weakness" (Swahili proverb). There are many Scriptures that illustrate the importance of unity and power of numbers. The discussion of the three-fold cord being difficult to break in Ecclesiastes 4:9–12 is similar in meaning to the above three Tanzanian proverbs. I appreciate the fact that the biblical Scripture enlightens the reader of the importance of individuals working together in unity. Further, the illustration informs that "two is better than one." Just think, if normal body temperature in humans is approximately 98.6 degrees Fahrenheit, two individuals combining their heat is much better that one. Try entering a cool room with just one other person. Then gradually fill the room with additional people. Notice how rapidly the room temperature increases as the room fills.

Now, complete a simple experiment using sticks. First, try breaking just one stick. Then gradually increase the number of sticks. You will find that it becomes more difficult to break the sticks as the number increases. Eventually, you will reach a point when they are unbreakable.

In a manner of speaking, the same principle applies with people. For example, in the time of war, a larger army is generally more victorious (providing artillery and competency are about the same). Of course, if God favors one side over the other, numbers, size, artillery, competency, and other factors are irrelevant. God alone is the majority and He is always victorious!

Ute Proverbs
———— and ————
Biblical Scriptures

"If I am in harmony with my family, that's success."
(Ute proverb)

*"And above all these things put on charity,
which is the bond of perfectness."*
(Colossians 3:14)

Read Colossians 3:12–17 and Psalm 133.

Comments:

Read the Scriptures and comments that accompany the following proverb which is found in the section on African proverbs:

"If relatives help each other, what evil can hurt them?" (African proverb).

How do you define success, and who determines if you are successful? That is a question each of us should ask. Otherwise, how will you know anything about your level of success. Since we are unique, I think the answer may be different for each of us. Have you ever heard the phrase "You can make some of the people happy some of the time, but you will never be able to make everyone happy?" I am confident that if you even try to make everyone happy, the first person to be unhappy will probably be you. So why would you consider allowing others to define success for you?

Generally, I set goals, objectives, and dreams very high for myself. I do not consider myself a failure if I do not reach all of my goals. In order to determine if I consider myself successful, I ask myself a number of questions. My level of success is quantified by my responses to the questions and how I feel about the responses.

One of the first questions I ask myself is "Would this be pleasing to God, or is it in His will?" Next, I would like to know if I am going to be happy with the outcome or if this aligns with the things I really want to do. It is also important to me to know that it aligns with the family goals and what we are striving to accomplish as a unit. Did I do my best? Will my outcome be a blessing to others?

After all the questions have been asked, I assess what was done. I do not ever consider myself a failure, even when outcomes are far from what I expected. Even when things do not go well, I believe God can use those events to work things out for our good.

Reflections: There were times when others would probably say things were not going well for my family. God blessed me to be the father of six daughters. The second child transitioned a few hours after birth. Before the oldest daughter completed high school, as a result of divorce, I was a single parent for eight years. Soon after the fifth daughter graduated from high school, she enrolled in college. There were times when four of the daughters, a son-in-law, and I were all in college at the same time (some in graduate school and some in undergraduate). Later, when the youngest daughter was in middle school, there were three in college. During the time the second daughter was in graduate school, the third daughter was teaching and taking additional graduate classes, and the youngest daughter was in undergraduate school, I had zero vision (which is still the case today, May 9, 2020). Yet, God saw us through it all. Sometimes, it was rough and tough, but God allowed us to work and live in harmony. With His guidance and help, we were able to be there for each other.

When I thought I would lose the home that is my current residence, God stepped in in the nick of time. When I finally made the last payment, I had been blind for two years. Today, I witness to the world that if families will trust God and work together, the sky is not the limit to what they can accomplish. There is no failure in God. Therefore, I decree, "No Limits! No Boundaries!"

Yoruba Proverbs
— and —
Biblical Scriptures

"By labor comes wealth."
(Yoruba proverb)

"Wealth gotten by vanity shall be diminished: But he that gathereth by labour shall increase."
(Proverbs 13:11)

*"Let him that stole steal no more:
But rather let him labour, working with his
hands the thing which is good,
that he may have to give to him that needeth."*
(Ephesians 4:28)

Read Micah 2:1–5 and 2 Thessalonians 3:10.

Comments:

There are many people either in jail or in the grave because they were determined to get wealth without working for it. Some have perpetrated elaborate scams, only to get caught and go to jail. Others try to steal their way to fortune. Instead, they find a new home in prison or the cemetery.

Paul, the apostle, in Ephesians 4:28, reminds the church that there needs to be a transformation from their previous ways. He reminded them that the appropriate way to obtain wealth is by labor. No doubt, Paul was aware of false prophets and others who engaged in schemes to obtain wealth without labor.

༺ৡৡ༻

"What you give, you get ten times over."
(Yoruba proverb)

"Give, and it shall be given unto you;
good measure, pressed down, and shaken together,
and running over, shall men give into your bosom.
For with the same measure that ye mete withal
it shall be measured to you again."
(Luke 6:38)

"I have shewed you all things, how that so laboring
ye ought to support the weak, and to remember
the words of the Lord Jesus, how He said, it is
more blessed to give than to receive."
(Acts 20:35)

Read Malachi 3:8–10.

Comments:

Have you ever met people who give, only because they are expecting something in return? I know individuals who say, "I'm going to plant this seed (financial blessing) because I need God to bless me with some money." Well, that is not the way to get a blessing from God. You should give out of love and knowledge that it is the right thing to do.

Money is not the only thing we should give. Sometimes the service, friendship, and kind words or deeds can be more valuable than money. Also, the love, joy, and happiness that one may experience through the giving and receiving of love is more valuable than riches.

Reflection: I recall a cousin who was mentally ill who gave me a quarter. At the time, I was her assistant pastor. She did not work, except taking care of her children. To date, that quarter remains one of the most rewarding gifts I ever received! I felt a tremendous sense of love and compassion as she presented it to me with a smile worth a million dollars!

༄༅༈

"The wealth which enslaves the owner isn't wealth."
(Yoruba proverb)

"For the love of money is the root of all evil: which while some coveted after, they have erred from the faith, and pierced themselves through with many sorrows."
(1 Timothy 6:10)

Comments:

Read the following proverbs and the Scriptures and comments that follow them in their perspective sections:

"Greed loses what it has gained" (African proverb).

"Money is sharper than the sword" (Ashanti proverb).

"You should not hoard your money and die of hunger" (Ghanaian proverb).

"Make some money, but don't let money make you" (Tanzanian proverb).

Zambian Proverbs
—————————— and ——————————
Biblical Scriptures

"When your luck deserts you, even cold food burns."
(Zambian proverb)

"Trust in the Lord with all thine heart; and lean not unto thine own understanding. In all thy ways acknowledge Him, and He shall direct thy paths."
(Proverbs 3:5–6)

Read Psalm 5:4, Psalm 32:1–5, Psalm 34:21, and Proverbs 28:1.

Comments:

Do not put your trust in luck or chance. Instead, put your trust in God. He is omnipotent, omnipresent, and omniscient. Nothing with Him is luck or chance. God will never leave or forsake us. He is not a deserter.

As a Christian, I take the opposite position of the above Zambian proverb. Even when things appear to be going bad, I feel that ultimately, they have to work out for my good (Romans 8:28). There is an Ashanti proverb that says, "You must act as if it is impossible to fail." Personally, I take that proverb a step further. Since I do not believe in luck, I try to "live as if it is impossible to fail." I trust that God will help me in all things. Therefore, since there is no failure in God, I do not accept failure as an option in me.

Zulu Proverbs

—— and ——

Biblical Scriptures

"The most beautiful fig may contain a worm."
(Zulu proverb)

*"But the Lord said unto Samuel, look not
on his countenance, or on the height of his stature;
because I have refused him: For the Lord seeth
not as man seeth; for man looketh on the outward
appearance, but the Lord looketh on the heart."*
(1 Samuel 16:7)

Read 1 Samuel 16:7–13.

Comments:

Review the following two proverbs in their respective sections with the accompanying Scriptures and comments:

"The skin of the leopard is beautiful, but not his heart" (Baluba proverb).

"A beautiful thing is never perfect" (Egyptian proverb). Man has a tendency to look at the outward appearance.

He often sees the beauty on the outside without realizing the ugly on the inside. Further, he fails to acknowledge that regardless of appearance, we all fall short of the glory of God. None of us are perfect. Perhaps, we are approaching maturity, but we are still imperfect.

"The rich are always complaining."
(Zulu proverb)

"He that loveth silver shall not be satisfied with silver;
nor he that loveth abundance with increase:
this is also vanity."
(Ecclesiastes 5:10)

"Wealth gotten by vanity shall be diminished: but
he that gathereth by labour shall increase."
(Proverbs 13:11)

Also, read Proverbs 13:8–12 and Luke 16:19–31.

Comments:

Do you ever pause to think about most of the world's wealth is in the hands of only a few people? One of the reasons for this is because the wealthy are never satisfied. It appears that they are so greedy that the more wealth they accumulate, the more they want. They are never satisfied because they are seeking the wrong riches. Individuals who seek spiritual wealth or riches and close relationships with God can find happiness and satisfaction even when they have limited physical or financial resources.

Those who seek first the kingdom of God and His righteousness learn to be thankful and happy with whatever resources are available to them. Like Paul, the apostle, they learn to be content, knowing that we can do all things through Christ which strengthens us (see Philippians 4:13). So whatever our state, whether limited resources or accumulated wealth, we learn to trust God with an assurance that He will meet all of our needs.

The rich who are always complaining are probably missing a relationship with God. Without Him in their lives, they will always have a void and never be satisfied. However, God wants us to have abundance, but we should share it and never forget to help the poor.

We should be grateful that in Christ Jesus, all true believers are spiritually rich. Man does not have the ability to rob us of our spiritual riches. Since our heavenly Father owns everything (see Psalm 24), as sons (heirs) we are benefactors and thereby wealthy. Accentuate the positive and do not allow anyone to deprive you of the joys of your wealth through Christ Jesus. Also, we should never consider ourselves as economically poor because we have a right to the physical blessings through Christ. When situations suggest dismal days, learn to lean and depend on Jesus. He will always make a way!

Exponential Growth: The Doubling Effect

From Pennies to Wealth in 27 Periods

Period 01	$0.02
Period 02	0.04
Period 03	0.08
Period 04	0.16
Period 05	0.32
Period 06	0.64
Period 07	1.28
Period 08	2.56
Period 09	5.12
Period 10	10.24
Period 11	20.48
Period 12	40.96
Period 13	81.92
Period 14	163.84
Period 15	327.68
Period 16	655.36

Period 17	1,310.72
Period 18	2,621.44
Period 19	5,242.88
Period 20	10,485.76
Period 21	20,971.52
Period 22	41,943.04
Period 23	83,886.08
Period 24	167,772.16
Period 25	335,544.32
Period 26	671,088.64
Period 27	$1,342,177.28

The above table was created to illustrate a simplistic approach to building wealth. It is important to understand that one does not require a large financial reserve in order to get started. Perhaps, the illustration is so simple that it appears too good to be true. However, even though it starts off with a minimal amount, as the periods progress, the goals are more difficult to achieve.

The idea is to come up with the ingenuity to progress from period to period. In the illustration, no details are given to show one how to accomplish each goal. That is where you have to put your mind and skills to work. However, in other manuscripts, I provide practical methods of doubling. Naturally, if you start off with a larger amount, you achieve your goal in fewer periods. Also, each person should make the project unique to their situation. Therefore, it is a good project, even for young children. You determine the length of each period. Finally, the periods do not have to be the same length and can be adjusted as needed

Printed in the United States
by Baker & Taylor Publisher Services